THE ORANGE TREE THEATRE PRESENTS

MONKEY'S UNCLE
BY DAVID LEWIS

AF075447

FIRST PERFORMED AT THE ORANGE TREE THEATRE, RICHMOND
ON 5 OCTOBER, 2005

MONKEY'S UNCLE
BY DAVID LEWIS

CAST

GEORGES FEYDEAU	DAVID LEONARD
MARIANNE FEYDEAU	AMANDA ROYLE
BENOIT DIDIER	STUART FOX
LOUIS LEVASSEUR	PAUL KEMP
CECILE HABILLOT	BETH CORDINGLY
ALPHONSE HABILLOT	ALISTER CAMERON
YVETTE	SAMANTHA DOWSON
DIRECTOR	SAM WALTERS
DESIGNER	VICKI FIFIELD
LIGHTING DESIGNER	KEVIN LEACH
ASSISTANT DIRECTORS	IMOGEN BOND
	AMY HODGE
STAGE MANAGER	STUART BURGESS
DEPUTY STAGE MANAGER	SOPHIE ACREMAN
PRODUCTION ASM	HANNAH WYE
SHOW ASM	STUART BURGESS
PRODUCTION TECHNICIANS	SARAH GOODA
	KEVIN LEACH

THE PLAYSCRIPT THAT FOLLOWS WAS CORRECT AT TIME OF GOING TO PRESS, BUT MAY HAVE CHANGED DURING REHEARSAL.

ALISTER CAMERON worked in the early days of the Orange Tree, when it was still in the room, in *The Sensation Novel, It Should Happen To a Dog, Trial By Jury, The Dock Brief,* and his own play *Kidneys,* which was the first production in the room after the opening of the new theatre. He has worked elsewhere: eight productions in the West End including *The Real Thing* at The Strand, *House Guest* at The Savoy, *Rolls-Hyphen-Royce* at The Shaftesbury and *No Sex Please, We're British* at The Strand. Many national and international tours as well as working extensively around the country. His television appearances include *Poirot, The Bill, London's Burning, Drop The Dead Donkey, Paul Merton The Series, The Harry Enfield Show* and made for TV films include *The Imitation Game, The Russian Bride, Words Of Love,* and *The Long Way Home*. For the past thirteen years Alister has run his own company, Richmond Productions, which tours English comedy theatre around the world.

BETH CORDINGLY Before training at Webber Douglas, Beth gained a double first in English and Drama from Birmingham University. Her first job was at the Orange Tree playing Desdemona in a schools' tour of *Othello*. In a tour to Canada she played Mary Magdalen in the *York Mystery Cycle*. Beth's first television role came soon after, as 17 year old wildchild Sara in *Family Affairs* (Channel Five). On quitting the soap Beth played juvenile lead Norma in Noel Coward's *Semi-Monde* (directed by Philip Prowse) at the Lyric, Shaftesbury Avenue. A film (*Two Men went to War*) and various television guest parts followed and then a stint as the popular but fated PC Kerry Young in ITV's *The Bill*. Beth can currently be seen in *Funland* (a new series for the BBC) playing Lancastrian pole-dancer Vienna Keen. She is thrilled to be working at the Orange Tree, and in theatre, again. Beth is also an ambassador for Childline.

SAMANTHA DOWSON trained at Mountview and the Drama Studio, London. She last appeared at the Orange Tree as Dolly Leete in *The Marrying of Ann Leete*. Previously she has appeared in *Saint's Day*, *Engaged*, *The Beggars Opera*, *The House of Bernarda Alba*, *The Mob*, *Doña Rosita the Spinster* and *Romeo and Juliet*. Other theatre work includes *The Speckled Band* and *Threepenny Opera* (Drayton Court Theatre), *As You Like It* and *Macbeth* (Bold and Saucy Theatre Company) and *Oliver Twist* (White Horse Theatre). Sam also appeared as Alice in *Alice in Wonderland* for Channel Four.

STUART FOX Previously at the Orange Tree Stuart has appeared in *The Game Hunter, The Three Sisters, Have you Anything to Declare?, The Caucasian Chalk Circle, The Way of the World, Sperm Wars, Court in the Act, Lips Together Teeth Apart, What the Heart Feels* and *Bodies*. Other recent theatre work includes *Drowning on Dry Land* (Scarborough), *Song of the Western Men* (Chichester), *Broken Glass* (Northampton Theatre Royal), *Confusions* (Salisbury Playhouse) and *The Illusion* (Royal Exchange Manchester). In the West End Stuart has appeared in *The Normal Heart* (Royal Court and Albery), *Filumena* (Lyric) and *Fear and Loathing in Las Vegas* (Fortune). Films include: *Return of the Jedi, Sid and Nancy* and *The Gospel of John*.

PAUL KEMP Theatre: *Private Fears in Public Places* (Stephen Joseph Theatre, Orange Tree Theatre, 59E59 Theaters New York), *Drowning On Dry Land* (Stephen Joseph and tour), *This Is Where We Came In, Hobson's Choice* (Stephen Joseph), *The Madness Of George III* (West Yorkshire Playhouse and Birmingham Rep), *The Absence Of War, Murmuring Judges, Racing Demon* (Birmingham Rep), *Way Upstream* (Derby Playhouse), *Naked Justice* (West Yorkshire Playhouse, Birmingham Rep and tour), *A Midsummer Night's Dream, Love's Labour's Lost, Much Ado About Nothing* (Open Air Theatre, Regent's Park), *A Wife Without A Smile, Lips Together Teeth Apart, Court In The Act, The Way Of The World, The Last Thrash, The Cassilis Engagement* (Orange Tree), *As You Like It, Obsession* (Battersea Arts Centre), *King Lear, The Rivals, Of Mice And Men, The London Merchant* (Southwark Playhouse). Television: *Life on Mars, Dream Team, TLC, Black Books, The Bill, On The Game*. Film: *When Saturday Comes*.

DAVID LEONARD trained at the Guildford School of Acting. At the Orange Tree David has appeared in *The Marrying of Ann Leete* and *Summer Again*. Other theatre credits include *Blithe Spirit* (Derby Playhouse), *Joking Apart* directed by Alan Ayckbourn (Stephen Joseph Theatre and tour), *Abandonment, Man of the Moment, The Wars of the Roses, The Way of The World, Private Lives, The Elephant Man* and *Hayfever* (Theatre Royal, York), *Popcorn* (Nottingham Playhouse, West Yorkshire Playhouse), *Servant of Two Masters* (Theatre Clwyd, Nottingham Playhouse), *Guys and Dolls* (National Tour), *Edward II, The White Devil, Richard III, The Crucible, When We Are Married, Single Spies,* and *Dolly West's Kitchen* (Leicester Haymarket), *Cowardy Custard* (Theatre Clwyd), *The Rivals* (Tour), seasons at

Mercury Theatre, Colchester and Redgrave, Farnham, *The Importance of Being Ernest* (Director, Theatre Royal York). Television: *Alice in Wonderland, A Scots Quair, Henry VI, Love is Forever*. Films: *Cracks, Hester, The Sun Also Rises, Comback*. Radio: *Strangers and Brothers, I Do Not Like Thee Dr. Fell, Playing for Time, D-Day*.

AMANDA ROYLE trained at the Central School of Speech and Drama. Orange Tree: *A Journey to London, Sauce for the Goose, Definitely the Bahamas, A Kind of Arden, No More a-Roving, All in the Wrong, Dissident, Winner Takes All* and *Hurting*. 1992/3 season: *The Dutch Courtesan, A Penny for a Song, Return of the Prodigal, The Artifice* and *Nice Dorothy*. 1998/9 Season: *Sperm Wars, Lips Together Teeth Apart, Court in the Act, The Way of the World, Low Flying Aircraft* and *The Cassilis Engagement*. More recently Amanda appeared in Feydeau's *The Game Hunter* and *Myth, Propaganda and Disaster in Nazi Germany and Contemporary America*. Other theatre includes *Rookery Nook, My Cousin Rachel, Blood Brothers* and *Oleanna* (Northampton Royal Theatre), *An Italian Straw Hat* (Shaftesbury Theatre), *Les Liaisons Dangereuses* (RSC, Ambassadors Theatre), *The New Menoza* (The Gate) and *Arcadia* (Library Theatre, Manchester). Television includes: *Lady Windermere's Fan, Miss Marple, Campion, Casualty, Devices and Desires, Poirot, Rides, The Bill, Secret House of Death, The Wingless Bird, Time Traveller, Staying Alive, Holby City, Doctors, Noah's Ark, The Jury, Dream Team, Touch of Frost* and *Rosemary & Thyme*. Films: *Two Deaths* and *All the Little Animals*.

SAM WALTERS took a degree at Oxford University, trained as an actor at LAMDA and then turned to directing with the formation of the Worcester Repertory Company. He was invited to form Jamaica's first full-time theatre company and drama school, and on his return to England in 1971 he founded the Orange Tree Theatre where his productions have ranged from Shakespeare through Restoration comedy to Feydeau and Brecht, as well as new plays by Crimp, Cregan, Havel, Saunders, Weldon, Wymark and David Lewis. He won a Time Out Award for his 1987/88 season and in 1991, the year the new theatre opened, the Orange Tree was awarded the Charrington Fringe Award for Outstanding Achievement in Small Theatre. He received the Peter Brook Empty Space Award for the work of 1992/93 company season. After directing the new theatre's opening production of *All in the Wrong* he seems to have directed about 40 productions in the new theatre and heaven knows how many before. Recently he directed *The Road to Ruin*, *Saint's Day, The Game Hunter, The Mob, King Cromwell, Love's a Luxury, The Marrying of Ann Leete* and *Myth, Propaganda and Disaster in Nazi Germany and Contemporary America*. He was awarded the MBE in 1999.

DAVID LEWIS David's plays *Bad Faith, Sperm Wars* (an earlier version of *Misconceptions*) and *Hurting* were all premiered at the Orange Tree Theatre between January 1998 and April 2000. He won a Pearson Bursary in 1999 for an attachment to the Orange Tree. *Misconceptions* has also been produced by the Bolton Octagon and the Derby and Salisbury Playhouses and by theatres in Finland, Denmark, Greece and New Zealand. In 2004, a Number One tour of *Misconceptions* starred Timothy Walker and Jemma Redgrave and was directed by Tim Carroll. For invaluable assistance during the writing of *Monkey's Uncle*, David would like to thank the following: Anne Short, George Hiken, Amanda Royle, Gwynne Lewis, Sam Walters and Georges Feydeau.

VICKI FIFIELD graduated from the Birmingham Institute of Art & Design with an MA in Scenography. She exhibited work in the Prague Quadrennial '99 (*The Tempest*) and was a first round finalist in the Linbury Prize for Stage Design. She is resident designer for Activated Image theatre company. Previous work includes *Peace* (Cockpit and touring), *The Learned Ladies* (Tristan Bates Theatre), *The Principle Of Motion* (Smirnoff Underbelly for Activated Image), *Lunch, When a Man Knows* and *Capital* (Kings Head), *Gates of Gold* (Finborough Theatre), *Patience* (Finborough for Activated Image), *The Gigli Concert* (Finborough and Assembly Rooms, Edinburgh). Vicki has designed various events at the National Theatre. She will be designing the forthcoming *Three in the Back, Two in the Head* also at the Orange Tree.

KEVIN LEACH trained at the Oldham College (entertainment technology and lighting and sound design). At the Orange Tree: *The Hebrew Lesson, Unsent Letters, Hippolytus, The Little Years, King Cromwell* and *Summer Again*. Extensive theatre credits in the north-west include: *Romeo and Juliet, The Merry Widow, Guys and Dolls, Billy Liar, Oklahoma!, Sweet Charity*, Willy Russell's *One for the Road, A Midsummer Night's Dream, Oliver!, Blood Brothers, The Lion, the Witch and the Wardrobe, Playhouse Creatures, Agamemnon* and *The Oldham Story* at the Queen Elizabeth Hall. He also worked as an ASM on the Commonwealth Games in Manchester. In 2002 Kevin lit *The Night Before Christmas* at the Riverside Studios, and recently *Amy Evans' Strike* at the Courtyard, Covent Garden.

ABOUT THE ORANGE TREE THEATRE

The Orange Tree Theatre opened on the 31 December 1971 in the upstairs room of the pub near to Richmond Station. It was part of the explosion of "alternative" theatre that blossomed in the late 60s and early 70s. It proved the right time and the right place, and having had to do the first lunchtime performance twice, to accommodate the numbers who came, the theatre developed throughout the 70s, often relishing the queues on the stairs eager for seats in those days before any form of booking at all!

In 1975 Young's Brewery renovated the pub and we moved from lunchtime to evening productions. **James Saunders** became a house playwright, writing *Bodies* for the theatre, as did **David Cregan**. The theatre produced a plethora of plays by **Vaclav Havel** and involved itself in Czech politics. The move towards the re-discovery of overlooked and forgotten plays began with *Dr. Knock* and *The Power of Darkness*. The musical *The Lady or The Tiger* and *The Primary English Class* transferred to the West End and there were the beginnings of a thriving schools programme.

The development continued in the 80s when we produced the first six plays of **Martin Crimp** and began a relationship with the French writer **Michel Vinaver**, six of whose plays we have now also produced. The 1987/1988 the season, which contained the premieres of Rodney Ackland's *Absolute Hell*, Harley Granville Barker's *The Secret Life* and John Whiting's *No More A-Roving*, won the theatre a Time Out Award. It was time to build the new theatre, which had been in the pipeline since the mid 70s.

The new Orange Tree Theatre, seating 172, London's only full time professional theatre in the round, opened in February 1991, in what had been a school, just across the road from the pub.

We had not begun in 1971 by intending to work only "in the round". But the first production, done by daylight at lunchtime, where the audience and the actors shared the space, clearly had its effect. When the possibility of creating a new theatre became concrete, we knew what we wanted. The Orange Tree is entirely committed to this form of theatre and all the productions are always in the round.

The policy of new plays, re-discoveries, foreign work and, occasionally, even in the round, musicals, has continued. **"A pocket sized National Theatre"** Michael Billington has written in *The Guardian*.

The schools work expanded and a highly successful trainee director scheme has been in operation since 1986, to which this year we have added a trainee writer.

There is always a desire to have a permanent company, whenever possible, and to nurture and develop relationships with actors, writers, directors and designers. Auriol Smith and Geoffrey Beevers, who have been involved with the theatre since the start, won Time Out Awards in the 1990s for *The Case of Rebellious Susan* and *Adam Bede* respectively. And as we approached 2000 we discovered an exciting new playwright in David Lewis. ***Monkey's Uncle*** is the fourth play of his we have premiered and all the cast have worked with the Orange Tree Theatre before.

Sam Walters *Artistic Director*

COMING NEXT

THREE IN THE BACK, TWO IN THE HEAD
By Jason Sherman **9 Nov – 10 Dec**
Directed by Adam Barnard
Designed by Vicki Fifield

"There are times when, for the good of the greater number, an individual must be sacrificed".

Donald Jackson, a weapons scientist for America's defence programme, is found dead outside a church. No witnesses, no motive. When his son goes to the CIA to attempt to piece together the truth about his father's death he is embroiled in a world of double agents, rogue states and global paranoia.

Inspired by the real-life murder of the Canadian weapons scientist Gerald Bull, *Three In The Back, Two In The Head* grapples with the elusive nature of truth as the action shifts across different versions of the past. Was Jackson a force for peace betrayed by hawkish politicians? Or was he on the cusp of giving America's greatest enemy the missile that could destroy it?

This searing examination of US military policy by one of Canada's foremost playwrights pits personal morality against the ambitions of the state. As President Bush ploughs yet more funds into a 'Star Wars' missile system to defend against 'the axis of evil', Sherman raises urgent questions about America's attempts to police the world.

Saturday Seminar: Canadian Theatre Now
With Jason Sherman.
Sat 3 Dec 10.30am £10 (£8 concessions)

A JOURNEY TO LONDON
By John Vanbrugh and James Saunders
14 Dec – 21 Jan, 6 – 11 Feb
Directed by Sam Walters
Designed by Sam Dowson

In the middle of his play, just as he had got his characters wound up and ready for the plot to take off, Restoration playwright John Vanbrugh put down his pen half way through a sentence and never wrote another word. James Saunders took this play about a country MP and his family coming to London, who then find themselves caught up in the wicked ways of the city, and created the most sophisticated of Restoration comedies for our times – sex and marriage 1700 style with twentieth century hindsight.

This delightful comedy, which was a huge success in the old theatre in 1986, is now revived as the central part of our tribute to the late James Saunders.

Birthday Performance: Sat 31 Dec 7pm £25
Ticket price includes a free glass of wine to toast the Theatre's 34th Anniversary.

Saturday Seminar:
The Plays of James Saunders
Early in his career James Saunders told an interviewer "If there's any theme that runs through my work, it's the absurdity of finding logic in anything at all." His first play that made a real impact on audiences and critics was the startling *Next Time I'll Sing to You*. It won him the 1963 *Evening Standard* Most Promising Playwright Award. Many of his plays were written for, and premiered at, the Orange Tree and this seminar is part of our celebration of his work.
Sat 28 Jan 10.30am £10 (£8 concesions)

A CELEBRATION OF JAMES SAUNDERS
Two Double Bills: 23 Jan – 4 Feb
James Saunders was a master of the short play and all 4 of these very different plays show him at the height of his powers.

GAMES AND AFTER LIVERPOOL
Games is an examination of war and conflict that makes truly unique demands on the audience.
After Liverpool is a delightful series of duologues about the impossibility of relationships.

BYE BYE BLUES AND DOUBLE DOUBLE
Bye Bye Blues shows three couples whose secure lifestyles and sense of liberty and freedom are threatened by a minor car accident. "It is quite simply a stunner" said *The Evening Standard* of our 1973 premiere.
Double Double is set in a bus garage where 5 actors play 10 parts as drivers and conductors grapple with timetables and a lost bus.

COMING NEXT

THREE IN THE BACK, TWO IN THE HEAD
By Jason Sherman **9 Nov – 10 Dec**
Directed by Adam Barnard
Designed by Vicki Fifield

"There are times when, for the good of the greater number, an individual must be sacrificed".

Donald Jackson, a weapons scientist for America's defence programme, is found dead outside a church. No witnesses, no motive. When his son goes to the CIA to attempt to piece together the truth about his father's death he is embroiled in a world of double agents, rogue states and global paranoia.

Inspired by the real-life murder of the Canadian weapons scientist Gerald Bull, *Three In The Back, Two In The Head* grapples with the elusive nature of truth as the action shifts across different versions of the past. Was Jackson a force for peace betrayed by hawkish politicians? Or was he on the cusp of giving America's greatest enemy the missile that could destroy it?

This searing examination of US military policy by one of Canada's foremost playwrights pits personal morality against the ambitions of the state. As President Bush ploughs yet more funds into a 'Star Wars' missile system to defend against 'the axis of evil', Sherman raises urgent questions about America's attempts to police the world.

Saturday Seminar: Canadian Theatre Now
With Jason Sherman.
Sat 3 Dec 10.30am £10 (£8 concessions)

A JOURNEY TO LONDON
By John Vanbrugh and James Saunders
14 Dec – 21 Jan, 6 – 11 Feb
Directed by Sam Walters
Designed by Sam Dowson

In the middle of his play, just as he had got his characters wound up and ready for the plot to take off, Restoration playwright John Vanbrugh put down his pen half way through a sentence and never wrote another word. James Saunders took this play about a country MP and his family coming to London, who then find themselves caught up in the wicked ways of the city, and created the most sophisticated of Restoration comedies for our times – sex and marriage 1700 style with twentieth century hindsight.

This delightful comedy, which was a huge success in the old theatre in 1986, is now revived as the central part of our tribute to the late James Saunders.

Birthday Performance: Sat 31 Dec 7pm £25
Ticket price includes a free glass of wine to toast the Theatre's 34th Anniversary.

Saturday Seminar:
The Plays of James Saunders
Early in his career James Saunders told an interviewer "If there's any theme that runs through my work, it's the absurdity of finding logic in anything at all." His first play that made a real impact on audiences and critics was the startling *Next Time I'll Sing to You*. It won him the 1963 *Evening Standard* Most Promising Playwright Award. Many of his plays were written for, and premiered at, the Orange Tree and this seminar is part of our celebration of his work.
Sat 28 Jan 10.30am £10 (£8 concesions)

A CELEBRATION OF JAMES SAUNDERS
Two Double Bills: 23 Jan – 4 Feb
James Saunders was a master of the short play and all 4 of these very different plays show him at the height of his powers.

GAMES AND AFTER LIVERPOOL
Games is an examination of war and conflict that makes truly unique demands on the audience. *After Liverpool* is a delightful series of duologues about the impossibility of relationships.

BYE BYE BLUES AND DOUBLE DOUBLE
Bye Bye Blues shows three couples whose secure lifestyles and sense of liberty and freedom are threatened by a minor car accident. "It is quite simply a stunner" said *The Evening Standard* of our 1973 premiere.
Double Double is set in a bus garage where 5 actors play 10 parts as drivers and conductors grapple with timetables and a lost bus.

ABOUT THE ORANGE TREE THEATRE

The Orange Tree Theatre opened on the 31 December 1971 in the upstairs room of the pub near to Richmond Station. It was part of the explosion of "alternative" theatre that blossomed in the late 60s and early 70s. It proved the right time and the right place, and having had to do the first lunchtime performance twice, to accommodate the numbers who came, the theatre developed throughout the 70s, often relishing the queues on the stairs eager for seats in those days before any form of booking at all!

In 1975 Young's Brewery renovated the pub and we moved from lunchtime to evening productions. **James Saunders** became a house playwright, writing *Bodies* for the theatre, as did **David Cregan**. The theatre produced a plethora of plays by **Vaclav Havel** and involved itself in Czech politics. The move towards the re-discovery of overlooked and forgotten plays began with *Dr. Knock* and *The Power of Darkness*. The musical *The Lady or The Tiger* and *The Primary English Class* transferred to the West End and there were the beginnings of a thriving schools programme.

The development continued in the 80s when we produced the first six plays of **Martin Crimp** and began a relationship with the French writer **Michel Vinaver**, six of whose plays we have now also produced. The 1987/1988 the season, which contained the premieres of Rodney Ackland's *Absolute Hell*, Harley Granville Barker's *The Secret Life* and John Whiting's *No More A-Roving*, won the theatre a Time Out Award. It was time to build the new theatre, which had been in the pipeline since the mid 70s.

The new Orange Tree Theatre, seating 172, London's only full time professional theatre in the round, opened in February 1991, in what had been a school, just across the road from the pub.

We had not begun in 1971 by intending to work only "in the round". But the first production, done by daylight at lunchtime, where the audience and the actors shared the space, clearly had its effect. When the possibility of creating a new theatre became concrete, we knew what we wanted. The Orange Tree is entirely committed to this form of theatre and all the productions are always in the round.

The policy of new plays, re-discoveries, foreign work and, occasionally, even in the round, musicals, has continued. **"A pocket sized National Theatre"** Michael Billington has written in *The Guardian*.

The schools work expanded and a highly successful trainee director scheme has been in operation since 1986, to which this year we have added a trainee writer.

There is always a desire to have a permanent company, whenever possible, and to nurture and develop relationships with actors, writers, directors and designers. Auriol Smith and Geoffrey Beevers, who have been involved with the theatre since the start, won Time Out Awards in the 1990s for *The Case of Rebellious Susan* and *Adam Bede* respectively. And as we approached 2000 we discovered an exciting new playwright in David Lewis. ***Monkey's Uncle*** is the fourth play of his we have premiered and all the cast have worked with the Orange Tree Theatre before.

Sam Walters *Artistic Director*

MEMBERSHIP

The Orange Tree Theatre is a registered charity, and in order for us to offer quality, accessible theatre at affordable prices and to continue our education and outreach projects, we cannot survive purely on box office takings and public subsidy. Since it was founded in a room above a pub in 1971, the Orange Tree has depended on the generosity of its loyal audiences and members to ensure the security of its future. So far this support has meant that not only could the theatre move to its own premises in 1991, but it has also acquired and transformed a former Bank Building into comfortable and productive workshop and rehearsal space.

With the Bank refurbishments now complete, the theatre's fundraising is now focused on the productions and our education programme.

PREVIEW CLUB (£25+)

For a suggested donation of £25 per year, you will receive:
- Monthly newsletter featuring news, special events, reviews and casting information
- Two tickets for the price of one at Preview performances (normally the first Wednesday and Thursday evening of each production)
- Priority booking

PRIVILEGE CLUB (£50+)

For a suggested donation of £50 per year, you will receive all of the benefits of Preview Club membership, as well as:
- Two tickets for each production with a 10% discount on full price or concession tickets
- Invitations to supporters evenings
- Open days and tours of the theatre
- Occasional special ticket offers

DONATIONS

There are many ways in which you can support the Orange Tree with a donation. Below is an idea of how your money can help us.

£5 will buy a prop

£10 will buy a script or vocal score

£20 will buy an item of costume

£50 will buy an item of furniture

£150 will help towards the theatre's technical equipment and will be acknowledged with your own plaque on the bar.

£250 will help towards the upkeep of the theatre building and will be acknowledged with your own plaque on a brick space in the Trevor Howard bar.

£500 will buy a seat space in the theatre complete with your own plaque.

The Orange Tree welcomes any donation, no matter how big or small, as everything helps to keep the theatre thriving without charging extortionate ticket prices. For every donation over £25, you will be entitled to DONATION CLUB MEMBERSHIP for one year, through which you will receive our monthly newsletter with news and features and advance information relating to all things Orange Tree.

To take advantage of our membership schemes contact:
Sarah Frain
Orange Tree Theatre
1 Clarence Street
Richmond, Surrey
TW9 2SA
Or call the Box Office on:
020 8940 3633

FOR THE ORANGE TREE

Orange Tree Theatre,
1 Clarence Street,
Richmond,
Surrey TW9 2SA
Tel: 020 8940 0141 (Admin)
Tel: 020 8940 3633 (Box Office)
Fax: 020 8332 0369
admin@orange-tree.demon.co.uk
www.orangetreetheatre.co.uk
Registered Charity 266128

Artistic Director	**Sam Walters**
Administrative Director	**Gillian Thorpe**
Financial Controller	**Joan Frost**
Administrative Assistant *(Education)*	**Ana Vrdoljak**
Administrative Assistant *(Fundraising)*	**Sarah Frain**
Administrative Assistant *(Press & Marketing)*	**Nick Budden**
Front of House Manager	**John Causebrook**
Box Office Supervisor and Duty Manager	**Charlotte Ive**
Stage Manager	**Stuart Burgess**
Stage Management	**Sophie Acreman**
	Sarah Gooda
	Kevin Leach
	Hannah Wye
Resident Design and Wardrobe	**Sam Dowson**
Trainee Directors	**Imogen Bond**
	Amy Hodge
Trainee Administrative Assistants	**Robert Alport**
	Francesca Clark
Trainee Writer	**Charlie Miller**
Audio Describer	**Veronika Hyks**
Youth Theatre Leaders	**Katie Henry**
	Vicky Shires
Bar Staff	**Gareth Evans**
	Caroline Glover
	Jackie Pankhurst
	Ben Upson
	Francesca Wilson

The Orange Tree would like to thank all volunteer ushers and programme sellers.

MONKEY'S UNCLE

by David Lewis

For Sam Walters
and the Orange Tree Theatre

CHARACTERS

Georges Feydeau (Act Three: George)

Marianne Feydeau (Act Three: Anne)

Benoit Didier (Act Three: Ben)

Louis Levasseur (Act Three: David)

Cécile Habillot (Act Three: Christine)

Alphonse Habillot (Act Three: Alan)

Yvette

ACT ONE

Paris, 1909. Early Afternoon. GEORGES FEYDEAU'S *study.*
FEYDEAU, *forty-six years old, is asleep under a sheet on a
chaise longue. He is wearing underwear only. The room is
something of a mess. There is a table, covered by a large
table cloth, on which there are various papers, pens, a pipe, a
large key, used coffee cups and a wine glass. (The table has a
small drawer.) There are a variety of chairs; a velvet smoking
jacket hangs on one of them.*

There are three exits: one to FEYDEAU'S *bedroom, one (or two)
to the rest of the house and one to the hall which leads to the
street. But all the doors are invisible. The actors mime the
opening and closing of doors with appropriate sound effects
provided by stage management.*

*We hear the beginning of the third movement ('Perpetuum
Mobile') of the Ravel Violin Sonata.* FEYDEAU *is sleeping,
apparently tormented by dreams.* YVETTE, *the maid, enters
from the hall. The music stops abruptly. Silently,* YVETTE
approaches FEYDEAU *and watches him with a sardonic smile.
She then looks around at the mess and her smile fades. She
notices the key on the table and picks it up, apparently
recognising it.*

MARIANNE   (*off*) Yvette?

          (*Pause.* YVETTE *taps* FEYDEAU *on the arm. No
response. She shakes his shoulder.*
FEYDEAU *wakes, unsure of where he is.*)

YVETTE   Monsieur, Madame is home.

          (FEYDEAU *begins to focus.* YVETTE *suppresses a
smile and leaves with the key.* FEYDEAU
*staggers to the bedroom door, opens it, and is
shocked by what he sees. He slams the door,
then regrets the noise. He tiptoes over to the
hall and peers out. He closes the door, tiptoes
back across the room and enters the bedroom,
closing the door behind him.* MARIANNE *enters
from the hall. She is forty years old,
attractive, well-dressed but seems stressed and*

rather unkempt. She sighs at the mess and begins tidying. Then she notices the papers on the table. She inspects them, frowning, then sits and begins to read. A child calls off.)

MARIANNE: In here, darling!

(She continues reading. Pause. The child calls again. She sighs and exits to the hall. FEYDEAU enters, half-dressed, and begins searching frantically. CÉCILE appears in doorway, wearing underwear and corset.)

FEYDEAU: How could you lose your dress?!

CÉCILE: *(searching the room)* It's here somewhere!

MARIANNE: *(off)* Georges?

FEYDEAU: *(panic)* My wife!

(CÉCILE is too far from the bedroom. She hides under the table. MARIANNE enters from the hall.)

FEYDEAU: Darling! You're home! Good morning!

MARIANNE: *(reproachful)* Good afternoon!

FEYDEAU: Yes! Indeed . . .

(He kisses her cheek. She allows it.)

FEYDEAU: How is auntie?

MARIANNE: Have you been drinking?

FEYDEAU: Perhaps a glass of wine.

MARIANNE: Carousing into the small hours again.

FEYDEAU: No, no, I was writing all night. With a fever. The muse took hold of me.

MARIANNE: Did she indeed? *(MARIANNE picks up some pages from the table.)*

FEYDEAU	I'd rather you didn't. It's very rough.
MARIANNE	(*reads*) 'Scruffy appearance: a dressing-gown with the cord trailing behind; a silk slip hanging over her nightdress; curlers in her hair; stockings drooping down onto shabby slippers. She is holding a slop pail full of water.'
FEYDEAU	I've borrowed some minor details.
MARIANNE	(*bitterly*) What a flattering portrait!
FEYDEAU	It's not you.
MARIANNE	(*stands in front of him*) Look at me! (*As he turns to look at her, she raises a hand to her hair and loses confidence in her appearance.*) No, look at that! (*Points randomly at something to divert his attention.*)
FEYDEAU	What?
MARIANNE	(*sees the wastepaper basket*) That!
FEYDEAU	That?
MARIANNE	Yes, that! That is my writing paper!
FEYDEAU	Oh. Yes, sorry. I ran out.
MARIANNE	Kindly remove it from the wastepaper basket.
FEYDEAU	It's been used.
MARIANNE	Both sides?
	(FEYDEAU *sighs and delves into the wastepaper basket.* MARIANNE *takes a tiny mirror from her dress and quickly adjusts her hair. Then she pulls up a stocking which has fallen onto her shoe.* FEYDEAU *removes a few relatively pristine pages from the basket and returns them to the table, blank side up.*)
FEYDEAU	It's just paper. I'll buy some more.

MARIANNE (*strikes a pose*) All right, look at me. (*He turns.*) Am I so repulsive?

FEYDEAU Not at all.

(*A moment between them.*)

CHILD (*off*) Mama!

MARIANNE All right, Jacques! They think they're not allowed in here.

FEYDEAU Of course they're allowed.

MARIANNE He's not been well again.

FEYDEAU Really? What's wrong?

MARIANNE Constipation. (FEYDEAU *sighs.*) Go and see him. Say hello.

FEYDEAU (*sits at the table*) I will. I just need to . . . I have an idea. (*He writes.*)

MARIANNE What have I said now?

FEYDEAU Sorry?

MARIANNE Every time we have an argument, you write it down.

FEYDEAU Nonsense.

MARIANNE You should pay me royalties!

FEYDEAU My dear, that's exactly what I've been doing ever since we were married.

(FEYDEAU *picks up his pipe and begins to fill it with tobacco as he studies his papers.* MARIANNE *picks up a luridly colourful scarf from the back of the chaise longue.*)

MARIANNE What is this?!

FEYDEAU   What d'you mean 'what is it'?

MARIANNE   WHOSE is it?

FEYDEAU   Mine. Of course. (*He takes it and puts it on.*) Do you like it?

           (*She stares at him. He puts on an ostentatious velvet smoking jacket.*)

MARIANNE   You're spending too much time in the theatre.

FEYDEAU   Perhaps.

MARIANNE   And why are you wearing odd socks?

FEYDEAU   Because you keep losing them!

MARIANNE   I'd buy some new ones. If we could afford it.

FEYDEAU   We can afford socks! Surely!

MARIANNE   Yes, if you didn't gamble all our money away!

FEYDEAU   Oh, nonsense . . .

MARIANNE   Auntie has a lawyer friend.

           (*Pause.*)

FEYDEAU   Funny how you keep bumping into lawyers.

MARIANNE   (*severe*) I'm resolved. If you continue to spend more time with harlots and drunkards . . .

FEYDEAU   Harlots?

MARIANNE   . . . than with your own family. If you continue to waste all our money on dining and gambling . . .

FEYDEAU   Dining?! A man has to eat!

MARIANNE Then I will instigate divorce proceedings. And you will be out of this house.

(*He stares at her, momentarily shaken.*)

FEYDEAU I'm doing my very best.

MARIANNE What were you up to last night? Drinking and gambling with Didier, the idiot doctor, I suppose.

FEYDEAU No, he doesn't gamble any more. Or drink.

MARIANNE Nonsense.

FEYDEAU He's a reformed man! I assure you.

(FEYDEAU, *feigning nonchalance, strikes a match for his pipe.* YVETTE *enters, followed by* DIDIER *who looks ill and dishevelled.*)

YVETTE Benoit Didier!

FEYDEAU (*aside*) Blast! How typical . . . (*He blows out the match.*)

DIDIER Good morning!

MARIANNE Good afternoon.

DIDIER Georges. Madame.

(*He kisses* MARIANNE'S *hand.* YVETTE *exits.*)

MARIANNE Goodness! You look awful!

DIDIER Yes, I have a headache. Sickness. And a fever, I think. But otherwise in fine fettle.

CHILD (*off*) Mama!

MARIANNE Coming! (*To* DIDIER.) Excuse me.

(DIDIER *bows with difficulty.* MARIANNE *exits to the hall, leaving the door open.*)

DIDIER   (*accusatory*) Where is Cécile?

FEYDEAU   Sshh! (FEYDEAU *peers into the hall then closes the door. He talks in a hushed voice.*) I've no idea. I remember nothing.

DIDIER   (*hushed also*) Nothing?! Not even Maxim's?

FEYDEAU   Benoit, I'm afraid you've caught me in the middle of something.

DIDIER   We left at one in the morning and you persuaded us back to your hotel room.

FEYDEAU   We went to the Hotel Terminus?!

DIDIER   Indeed we did. The four of us.

FEYDEAU   (*momentary panic*) Four?!

DIDIER   You, me, Cécile and the green fairy.

FEYDEAU   I don't drink absinthe.

DIDIER   You did last night.

FEYDEAU   That explains everything.

DIDIER   And you left me there!

FEYDEAU   Yes, it's coming back. You fell asleep.

DIDIER   (*louder*) In the bath!

FEYDEAU   Ssshh! (*A thought occurs.*) Where is my key?

DIDIER   Sorry?

FEYDEAU   (*searching through papers on the table*) My hotel key. Perhaps my wife found it . . . Blast!

DIDIER	You have your own key?
FEYDEAU	I have the room booked all week.
DIDIER	Really? Why?
FEYDEAU	(*continuing to search*) No reason . . . It's useful sometimes . . . Auditions and the like.
DIDIER	Well, anyway, why did you leave me there?

(MARIANNE *enters unheard from the house.*)

FEYDEAU	Where?
DIDIER	The hotel! I woke up an hour ago and found myself lying in a bath!

(FEYDEAU *looks up and sees* MARIANNE *standing behind* DIDIER.)

DIDIER	The tap dripping onto my hat woke me up!
MARIANNE	No wonder you've a headache.

(DIDIER *jumps. Casually,* MARIANNE *collects some used cups and a wine glass.*)

DIDIER	Oh, it's nothing! Just . . . a head cold, perhaps.
MARIANNE	Or a hangover.
FEYDEAU	Surely not! You don't drink any more. Do you?
DIDIER	No. Indeed. I abstain, as far as possible . . .
MARIANNE	Why were you asleep in a bath?
DIDIER	(*beat*) Well, I was very tired. I visited Monsieur Forfilier. The Minister for the Navy. He has an abscess. I arrived home very late, got into the bath and just . . . fell asleep!

MARIANNE	Fully clothed?
DIDIER	Er . . . No, no! No, I bathe . . . as nature intended. If you'll pardon . . .
MARIANNE	You said the tap dripping onto your hat woke you up.
DIDIER	Yes. Indeed. I . . . forget to remove it after my visit. To the Minister.
MARIANNE	You got into the bath, perfectly sober, in a top hat!
DIDIER	A top hat?! No, no! Not at all. No, a . . . um . . . A bathing hat. (*Smile.*) All right, I confess! I was wearing my wife's floral bathing cap!
MARIANNE	To visit the Minister for the Navy?!
DIDIER	No! Good heavens! No, no, I wear it in the bath. On occasion. I admit it looks rather absurd. But it serves it's purpose.
FEYDEAU	My dear, have you finished your cross-examination?
DIDIER	Always a pleasure. (*He bows to her. A pause.*)
MARIANNE	(*swallows her anger*) Well, I'll leave you of course. Naturally you'll need a few moments to invent a story that's remotely believable.
	(*Exit* MARIANNE *to the house.*)
FEYDEAU	(*annoyed, hushed*) That was such a poor performance!
	(DIDIER *begins clearing some space on the chaise longue in order to sit down.*)
DIDIER	I am not on top form! And it's your fault! The green fairy was your idea!

(DIDIER *discovers* CÉCILE'S *dress.* FEYDEAU *snatches it from him before he has a chance to recognise it.*)

FEYDEAU Ah! That's mine! I mean . . . my wife's . . . She lost it. (DIDIER *stares.*) All right, I confess! I sometimes wear my wife's dress. To visit the Minister for the Navy.

DIDIER (*coldly*) Yes, very droll.

FEYDEAU I'm spending too much time in the theatre.

DIDIER Georges, I need her. Cécile. I've been ill. Since I lost her.

FEYDEAU Drunk, at least.

DIDIER It was the worst decision I ever made!

FEYDEAU I thought she left you.

DIDIER Yes! Because I wouldn't commit. I behaved like a coward!

FEYDEAU You are a coward.

DIDIER Yes! Which explains my behaviour! But she wouldn't accept that. She threatened to speak to my wife.

FEYDEAU Goodness.

DIDIER If I did not speak to her husband.

FEYDEAU Why should you?

DIDIER She wants me to confront him! To prove myself!

FEYDEAU Why doesn't she speak to him?

DIDIER	She did! She asked for a separation! But he won't allow it! He's a police inspector.
FEYDEAU	Yes. I know.
DIDIER	(*rises and paces, anxiously*) A very large police inspector.
FEYDEAU	Large?
DIDIER	Tall.
FEYDEAU	I see.
DIDIER	Much like my wife. Tall. Imposing.
FEYDEAU	(*preparing his pipe*) Benoit, I really must work.
DIDIER	Piercing eyes. Bald as a coot.
FEYDEAU	Your wife?!
DIDIER	No! The inspector! And he's much older than her. It's hardly a marriage. In the proper sense.
FEYDEAU	Benoit . . .
DIDIER	But he's possessive, apparently. Jealous. Volatile.
	(*Irritated by* DIDIER'S *pacing,* FEYDEAU *rises, pipe in hand, and takes his arm.*)
FEYDEAU	Benoit, I'm awfully sorry, but . . .
DIDIER	(*notices the scarf around* FEYDEAU'S *neck*) Cécile has a scarf like that. Perhaps she acquired it to copy you.
FEYDEAU	Perhaps.
	(FEYDEAU *removes it.* DIDIER *takes it.*)

DIDIER She's so impressed by you. The way you dress. (*He tries on the scarf.*) The way you talk. And she loves your plays of course. Did I tell you she's a very fine actress?

FEYDEAU Many times.

DIDIER It is so difficult for a cabaret singer to break out of that world. She'd love to audition for you. At your convenience.

(FEYDEAU *collects a match for his pipe.*)

FEYDEAU Certainly. When I'm rather less busy . . . (DIDIER *begins crying.*) Benoit . . . For heaven's sake . . . (FEYDEAU *blows out the match.*)

DIDIER It's torture! I never see her enough! I never know how to see her! Where to see her!

FEYDEAU Your wife's away, isn't she?

DIDIER Yes, but always liable to turn up . . .

FEYDEAU Yes, wives do that . . .

DIDIER I have no choice! I must talk to her husband!

FEYDEAU Is that wise?

DIDIER (*clearly anxious*) He's a professional man! He'll see sense! Surely!

(FEYDEAU *takes* DIDIER *aside, away from the table.* DIDIER *looks around, rather confused.*)

FEYDEAU Do you intend to marry this girl?

DIDIER Why not?

FEYDEAU Her days at the Folies-Bergère . . . Or, should I say, her nights. There are many stories . . .

DIDIER   What stories?!

FEYDEAU   You heard them too! In fact, you told me some of them! They excited you! But an exciting girl does not make a suitable wife.

DIDIER   Why not?

FEYDEAU   Because excitement lasts for twelve months. Thereafter you need someone who isn't going to lose your socks. (*Leads him towards the hall.*) Anyway, I apologise, but I really must continue . . .

DIDIER   Georges, I treat royalty! The glittering elite! Only last week I attended to the Countess of Castillon's gout. And I can assure you Madame Habillot has more sophistication than any woman I have ever met! She is the jewel in my crown!

                (CÉCILE *emerges from under the table.*)

CÉCILE   That's so sweet of you.

                (*Beat.*)

DIDIER   (*shocked*) What were you doing under there?!

FEYDEAU   Cécile, please!

                (FEYDEAU *moves to one door and then another to verify his wife's whereabouts.*)

DIDIER   Have you no shame?! Hiding under the table like a cheap tart?!

CÉCILE   How dare you?!

DIDIER   What is going on here?!

FEYDEAU   I slept on the chaise. She slept in there.

DIDIER	In your bed?!
CÉCILE	It was perfectly innocent!
	(FEYDEAU *begins to gather up* CÉCILE'S *clothes.*)
FEYDEAU	You must leave! Immediately!
DIDIER	Now I see why you advise me against confronting Monsieur Habillot!
FEYDEAU	(*hands* CÉCILE'S *purse to her*) Oh! Do you have my hotel key?
DIDIER	And why, whenever we dine together, you insist I bring Cécile!
FEYDEAU	Keep your voice down!
DIDIER	Well, that's that! I'll confront Monsieur Habillot! As soon as possible!
YVETTE	(*enters*) Monsieur Habillot!
FEYDEAU	Naturally . . .
	(DIDIER *ducks under the table.* CÉCILE *tries to evict him.*)
CÉCILE	Benoit! That's my place!
DIDIER	There's no room!
CÉCILE	Have you no manners?!
FEYDEAU	Bedroom! (*Panicking, he tries to pull her towards the bedroom.*)
CÉCILE	No! I will not hide! Like a cheap tart!
	(*She sits defiantly on the chaise longue.*)
FEYDEAU	You're not dressed!

HABILLOT   (*enters*) Monsieur! It's a great honour!

            (FEYDEAU – *with his back to* HABILLOT – *holds up the sheet to obscure* CÉCILE, *then throws it over her head so that it covers her entirely.*)

FEYDEAU   Ah!

HABILLOT   Ah!

FEYDEAU   (*theatrically*) "A-ha! The lady in question!" (*To* CÉCILE:) "Do not fear, Madame. I will respect your secrecy!"

HABILLOT   Monsieur?

FEYDEAU   "I merely wish to know if Doctor Moricet is here." (*He sighs.*) Shake your head! You're supposed to shake your head! (*He turns to* HABILLOT.) Monsieur Habillot. (*Shakes his hand.*) Delighted to meet you. We'll be finished shortly. (*Turns to* YVETTE *who has been watching, fascinated.*) Yvette, that will be all.

            (YVETTE *raises her eyes and exits to the hall.*)

HABILLOT   I'm very sorry to impose. A waiter at Maxim's told me you might know the whereabouts of my wife.

FEYDEAU   I do indeed.

            (FEYDEAU *removes the sheet.*)

CÉCILE   Hello, darling.

HABILLOT   Goodness!

FEYDEAU   We're rehearsing. A revival. The Game Hunter.

HABILLOT   Rehearsing . . . ?

FEYDEAU	Well, more an audition than a rehearsal. Never mind. We'll continue later.
	(*Causally*, FEYDEAU *collects* CÉCILE'S *dress and hands it to her. She dresses quickly.*)
HABILLOT	Cécile! You're not decent!
FEYDEAU	She's properly attired. For the role.
HABILLOT	I beg your pardon, Monsieur, but I'm shocked.
CÉCILE	Please excuse Alphonse. He's rather inhibited about the human body.
HABILLOT	Inhibited?
FEYDEAU	Monsieur, I demand verisimilitude. If the play stipulates underwear, then we rehearse in underwear.
HABILLOT	Really? Well, I suppose . . . I take the same approach to crime scene reconstructions.
FEYDEAU	You do them in underwear?
HABILLOT	No, no. I do them with as much accuracy as possible.
FEYDEAU	I see.
HABILLOT	A crime of passion might well entail underwear.
FEYDEAU	Yes. I'm sure. For example, if your wife keeps losing your socks.
	(CÉCILE *checks the contents of her purse. She finds a large key identical to the one* YVETTE *picked up.*)
HABILLOT	Yes . . . Well, that's not really what I meant.

(FEYDEAU *unfurls the sheet then kicks* DIDIER *under the table.* HABILLOT *turns to* CÉCILE *who quickly returns the key to her purse.*)

HABILLOT (*sits*) Cécile, I'm surprised you didn't tell me.

CÉCILE I wanted it to be a surprise, darling. I slipped out early this morning.

(FEYDEAU *ushers* DIDIER *out of the room by kicking his backside through the sheet as he folds it up.*)

HABILLOT I wasn't even sure that you'd been home.

CÉCILE Oh, yes, of course. I try not to wake you.

FEYDEAU (*aside, as* DIDIER *is ejected to the hall*) Good riddance!

HABILLOT Well, I'm very sorry to interrupt . . .

FEYDEAU Don't worry. We'll continue some other time.

CÉCILE (*eagerly*) Really? When?

FEYDEAU Er . . .

CÉCILE I have a couple of monologues prepared . . . Both yours, in fact. The Woman Condemned to Death and The Woman Who Hates Monologues. That's my favourite.

FEYDEAU The *Woman* Who . . . ?

CÉCILE Yes, I changed the gender. I hope you don't mind. I performed them recently at a charity concert for unmarried mothers.

FEYDEAU (*under-whelmed*) Indeed.

HABILLOT (*re: the papers*) Are you writing a new play?

FEYDEAU	Yes. But stuck, as usual. And it's always endings. Beginnings are easy. But endings are painful. Don't you find?
	(DIDIER *returns from the hall, still wearing* CÉCILE'S *scarf. His hair is a mess.*)
DIDIER	Monsieur! (*They look.*) I have something to say . . . (HABILLOT *stands. Confronted by* HABILLOT'S *size,* DIDIER'S *courage fails.*) Um . . .
FEYDEAU	No, no. Come on. Out!
	(FEYDEAU *manhandles him back out of the room.*)
DIDIER	(*off*) Cécile, I want you! I need you!
HABILLOT	What did he say? (FEYDEAU *returns.*) Did he say 'I need you'?
FEYDEAU	Yes. 'I need you . . . back at the Folies-Bergère.' He is an impresario. Hence the . . . flamboyant clothing.
CÉCILE	And the ridiculous hair-style.
HABILLOT	Why did you throw him out?
FEYDEAU	I think you should decline him, Cécile. Cabaret is beneath you. Your future is in the theatre.
CÉCILE	You really think so?
HABILLOT	Perhaps he'd take me instead.
FEYDEAU	Sorry?
HABILLOT	I have a novelty act.
CÉCILE	(*privately*) Not now, darling.

HABILLOT   Would you mind, Monsieur?

CÉCILE   Alphonse . . .

HABILLOT   Perhaps an excerpt from Dawn at the Farmyard . . .

(HABILLOT *begins with a loud impression of a cockerel and then mimics a variety of farmyard animals in quick succession. He is quite good and seems to have no capacity for embarrassment.* CÉCILE *watches, irritated.* MARIANNE *enters from the house with a disturbed expression.* YVETTE *enters from the hall and seems to enjoy the performance.* FEYDEAU *stands motionless, slightly startled.* HABILLOT *finishes and bows.*)

YVETTE   Bravo!

(YVETTE *applauds which causes others to applaud with less enthusiasm.*)

FEYDEAU   Extraordinary.

HABILLOT   Just a brief melange. What do you think?

YVETTE   You're very talented, Monsieur!

FEYDEAU   Prodigiously.

MARIANNE   That will be all, Yvette. Thank you.

(*After a moment's defiance,* YVETTE *curtsies and exits.*)

FEYDEAU   My dear! May I introduce Monsieur and Madame Habillot?

CÉCILE   Madame. Delighted to meet you.

MARIANNE   Cécile Salvigne?

CÉCILE   Ah! You know me?!

MARIANNE   By reputation.

HABILLOT   Enchanted.

(*He kisses her hand.*)

MARIANNE   You have a . . . unique act, Monsieur.

HABILLOT   Thank you! But I'm not sure if there's an audience for it.

FEYDEAU   In Paris there is an audience for everything.

HABILLOT   I've performed at various soirées. A full hour for the Mayor of Moussagnac.

FEYDEAU   Goodness.

HABILLOT   There are a number of successful impressionists in Paris.

FEYDEAU   I believe Le Petomane does animal impressions nightly at the Theatre Pompadour.

HABILLOT   Le Petomane? He breaks wind!

FEYDEAU   Yes, in the manner of . . . a goose, for example.

MARIANNE   A goose breaking wind?!

FEYDEAU   No, no. He affects the call of the goose by discharging air from his . . .

CÉCILE   I saw him perform at the Moulin Rouge.

HABILLOT   Really?!

CÉCILE   Many years ago . . . (*Smile.*) I remember he finished with a rendition of the Marseillaise!

MARIANNE   He sang it?

CÉCILE   No. I'm afraid not.

HABILLOT	Well, that's disgraceful!
CÉCILE	It was most amusing.
HABILLOT	No, no, I'm sorry. I hold to the opinion that every public performance of the Marseillaise must be rendered by the mouth alone.
CÉCILE	Perhaps I could do a quick monologue . . .

(YVETTE *returns from the hall.*)

YVETTE	Monsieur Louis Levasseur!
FEYDEAU	Oh, not again.

(LEVASSEUR *bursts in from the hall brandishing a battered script.*)

LEVASSEUR	Georges, I have it! The ending for my play! Do you mind . . . ?
MARIANNE	(*eagerly*) Not at all.
FEYDEAU	I need to write my own ending.
LEVASSEUR	(*looking around*) Am I interrupting . . . ?

(YVETTE *exits.*)

FEYDEAU	Monsieur and Madame Habillot.
HABILLOT	(*bows*) We should be going . . .
CÉCILE	No, I'd like to hear the gentleman's idea. (*To* LEVASSEUR.) If you don't mind . . .
LEVASSEUR	No, indeed.
CÉCILE	I am an actress.
LEVASSEUR	Ah! Yes, I can see that. Your natural deportment. (CÉCILE *smiles.* MARIANNE

assesses Cécile *with a frown.*) In fact, you look very much like Angelique, my heroine.

CÉCILE Do I?

FEYDEAU Louis, I'm actually rather busy . . . (*He adds more tobacco to his pipe.*)

LEVASSEUR Sorry! I'll be swift. The suit is the murder weapon!

FEYDEAU The suit?!

LEVASSEUR (*excited*) His new suit! The very symbol of his social advancement!

FEYDEAU How do you murder someone with a suit?

LEVASSEUR His belt! He strangles Chambraud with his belt!

FEYDEAU Melodramatic.

LEVASSEUR Not at all! It works perfectly! (*To* Cécile.) Madame, may I borrow you briefly?

CÉCILE Certainly.

LEVASSEUR Georges, you are Chambraud.

FEYDEAU (*strikes a match*) I'm afraid I don't have time.

LEVASSEUR Just turn your chair for a moment. (*He blows out* Feydeau's *match and helps him turn his chair around.*) Angelique is sitting on your knee. (*To* Habillot.) Do you mind, Monsieur?

HABILLOT Not at all. Is she fully-clothed? (Cécile *sits on* Feydeau's *knee.*)

LEVASSEUR Er . . . No. Not entirely.

HABILLOT I am a policeman. I am familiar with murder. And underwear.

FEYDEAU	Get on with it.

LEVASSEUR	(*to* HABILLOT) My hero, Emile, works in a clothing factory. He believes it is his industry, his ability, which has caused his elevation through the hierarchy. He does not know that there is another reason! He does not know of his wife's noble, or ignoble, sacrifice.

HABILLOT	I see.

LEVASSEUR	He has money. He has self-respect. He has bought his first suit. He knows that his mother, a poor seamstress, may have worked on the very suit he now wears. She would receive almost nothing of the large sum he has paid to buy it. But he tries to dismiss her from his mind. In his excitement with his new identity, he enters, without knocking, the office of Monsieur Chambraud, his patron, his mentor . . . (LEVASSEUR *moves into space and approaches* FEYDEAU *who is facing away from him.*) And he discovers his young wife . . . on the knee of Chambraud. A murderous rage engulfs him! He removes his fine jacket. (*He removes his own shabby jacket.*) He removes his leather belt . . . (*He removes his cheap belt.*) He approaches Chambraud . . . (*He approaches* FEYDEAU, *his belt taut between two fists.*)

FEYDEAU	And his trousers fall down.

	(CÉCILE *and* HABILLOT *laugh.*)

HABILLOT	Excellent! (*To* LEVASSEUR.) Write that down.

LEVASSEUR	I am a serious dramatist. I do not deal in such frivolities.

FEYDEAU	(*helping* CÉCILE *to her feet*) Life itself is frivolous.

LEVASSEUR	(*wielding his script*) This is a serious play. About the ordinary people of Paris. The disenfranchised. And I need a theatre.
FEYDEAU	Your place is in the people's theatre.
MARIANNE	There is no 'people's theatre' any more! You know very well. Just endless cabaret, circuses. And now those absurd cinemas!
LEVASSEUR	As Zola said: the rallying cry of the crowd is always 'Lower! Lower!'
MARIANNE	Absolutely!
FEYDEAU	(*irritated*) What is this crowd? Who comprises the crowd?
LEVASSEUR	I beg your pardon?
FEYDEAU	The crowd is the public, Monsieur Levasseur. The ordinary people of Paris.
LEVASSEUR	Indeed.
FEYDEAU	I thought you were for the people.
LEVASSEUR	(*hesitant*) I am. For the people. In spite of the people.
FEYDEAU	I see.
LEVASSEUR	At least my plays are not mindless entertainment.
FEYDEAU	I beg your pardon?
LEVASSEUR	At least they have some sort of message.
FEYDEAU	Yes, 'Don't go to the theatre'! That's the message!

(*The* HABILLOTS *laugh.* LEVASSEUR *puts on his jacket.*)

LEVASSEUR	(*grandly*) Fine. Laugh all you like! But I know one thing! I know that the name Louis Levasseur will be remembered . . .
CÉCILE	Who?
LEVASSEUR	Me, madame! My name will be enshrined for posterity whereas yours, Georges Feydeau, will be entirely forgotten!
	(*He turns to leave and his trousers fall down. He trips over them and falls onto his face.*)
FEYDEAU	Bravo!
	(*The* HABILLOTS *laugh louder.* LEVASSEUR *leaves, wrestling with his trousers and his script which is falling apart.*)
MARIANNE	(*incensed*) How dare you laugh?! That man is a great dramatist! And you make noises like a pig!
FEYDEAU	Marianne!
MARIANNE	Go back to the farm, Monsieur! Where you belong! Go and live with the pigs! It might improve your act!
HABILLOT	My darling, we must leave! (*He bows to* FEYDEAU.) Good day, Monsieur!
	(*He exits to the hall.* MARIANNE *follows.*)
MARIANNE	(*as she goes*) Yvette! The Habillots are leaving!
HABILLOT	(*off*) Cécile!
CÉCILE	I found a key. (*She takes it out of her purse.*)
FEYDEAU	Ah! Much obliged.

CÉCILE	But only one. Should I keep it?
FEYDEAU	Keep it?
CÉCILE	It's a spare, isn't it? You gave it to me. You said it might make life a bit easier.
FEYDEAU	(*takes the key*) No, no, I'm afraid I need it.
CÉCILE	(*rejected*) What about my monologue?
HABILLOT	(*off*) Cécile!!
FEYDEAU	You should go. (*He turns away.*)
CÉCILE	(*suddenly, and with volume*) "I am condemned to death! At my age!"
FEYDEAU	Sssshhhh!
CÉCILE	"So young! So intelligent! So beautiful!"
FEYDEAU	Not now! For heaven's sake . . . !

(*He ushers her out. She almost collides with* MARIANNE *in the doorway.* FEYDEAU *puts the key in his pocket.*)

MARIANNE	(*suspicious*) What was that? Did she give you something?
FEYDEAU	What on earth's the matter with you?
MARIANNE	I will not have that woman in my house!
FEYDEAU	Why ever not?
MARIANNE	Cécile Salvigne?! She's a well known society whore!
FEYDEAU	Malicious gossip! And her name is Cécile Habillot. Her husband is a Police Inspector!

MARIANNE	(*unimpressed*) Really? I took him for a pig farmer.
	(FEYDEAU *sighs and sits at the table with his back to* MARIANNE. *She sees an opportunity to pick his pocket and moves silently towards him. But* FEYDEAU *turns as she approaches.*)
FEYDEAU	I need to work.
MARIANNE	Will you be at home tonight? With your family.
FEYDEAU	I need to visit the theatre briefly. (*He begins adding more tobacco to his pipe.*)
MARIANNE	Do you? And then the Napolitain? And then Maxim's?
FEYDEAU	No. I'll be straight home. Nine at the latest.
MARIANNE	(*sceptical*) Really? Well, that would save us some money at least!
	(DIDIER *enters tentatively from the hall. He bows to* MARIANNE.)
MARIANNE	I thought you'd gone.
DIDIER	Er . . . Yes. Presently. I'm just returning a scarf.
	(*He takes off* CÉCILE'S *scarf and hands it to* FEYDEAU.)
FEYDEAU	Thank you.
MARIANNE	(*suddenly*) How is Bertha?
DIDIER	(*momentarily thrown*) Bertha?
MARIANNE	Your wife.
DIDIER	Yes. I wasn't aware . . .

MARIANNE	Do you often forget that you're married?
FEYDEAU	(*tending to his pipe*) Marianne, why do you always sound like a barrister?
DIDIER	I wasn't aware that you knew her.
MARIANNE	I met her some time ago. We share the same milliner.
DIDIER	Fancy that!
MARIANNE	I must arrange coffee some time.
DIDIER	Yes! Well, she's away at the moment. With her sister.
MARIANNE	How convenient.
FEYDEAU	Objection, your honour!
DIDIER	(*joins in the joke*) Sustained!

(*He quickly takes* FEYDEAU'S *pipe and bangs it on the table as if it's a gavel. The pipe's contents are scattered over the table. Heavy pause.* MARIANNE *stares at him with utter contempt.*)

DIDIER	I'm terribly sorry. (*He begins, rather incompetently, to clear up the mess.*)
MARIANNE	No. Leave it. (*She sweeps it expertly with one hand into the other. Under her breath:*) I spend my life clearing up after children. Big ones and little ones.

(MARIANNE *exits to the hall.*)

DIDIER	(*hushed*) What happened? (FEYDEAU *stares.*) With Habillot.
FEYDEAU	Don't worry. He didn't hear.

DIDIER	I intended him to hear.
FEYDEAU	Have you talked to him? At all?
DIDIER	No. What's he like?
	(FEYDEAU *looks around, aware that* MARIANNE *might reappear from any door.*)
FEYDEAU	Mad. Very clearly.
DIDIER	Mad?!
FEYDEAU	Well . . . Bordering on insanity.
DIDIER	(*anxious*) Georges, don't exaggerate, please! Because mental illness is not funny!
FEYDEAU	Indeed not.
DIDIER	My grandfather suffered all his life. Ended up believing he was a bird. A pigeon, in fact.
FEYDEAU	A pigeon?!
DIDIER	His death was very . . . traumatic for the whole family.
FEYDEAU	He fell off his perch?
DIDIER	Please don't joke! I beseech you!
FEYDEAU	(*removes his jacket and rolls up his sleeves*) I really must work.
DIDIER	Shall I see you later at Maxim's?
FEYDEAU	No, I need to be home early. (FEYDEAU *studies his papers.*)
DIDIER	(*beat*) Perhaps tomorrow night. (DIDIER *rises to leave but hesitates.*) Georges, tell me the truth. Do you have designs on Cécile?

FEYDEAU Not at all!

DIDIER I'm aware that I can't compete with you.

FEYDEAU Nonsense.

(DIDIER *picks up* FEYDEAU'S *jacket and tries it on.*)

DIDIER Even the best clothes scarcely improve my appearance.

FEYDEAU Why do you have to try on all my clothes?

DIDIER Cécile told me I dress like her grandfather. Does this suit me?

FEYDEAU Can I have that back, please?

DIDIER I'm so confused! Maybe, if you took her off my hands, I'd be a happier man!

FEYDEAU I have no intention of taking her off anyone's hands! (*Reaching for the jacket.*) Benoit, my jacket . . .

(*Before* FEYDEAU *can reclaim the jacket,* YVETTE *enters at speed from the hall.*)

YVETTE Monsieur Levasseur's been robbed! In broad daylight!

DIDIER Robbed?!

FEYDEAU He barely owns anything.

YVETTE They stole his script!

FEYDEAU What a senseless crime!

(LEVASSEUR *staggers into the room, assisted by a concerned* MARIANNE.)

MARIANNE	Didier, quick! Help him onto the bed!
LEVASSEUR	(*semi-conscious*) I'm perfectly fine!
	(MARIANNE, YVETTE *and* DIDIER (*still wearing* FEYDEAU'S *jacket*) *guide* LEVASSEUR *into the bedroom.*)
FEYDEAU	Not in there! He's filthy!
	(FEYDEAU *mutters something under his breath and returns to his papers.* CÉCILE *enters from the hall.*)
CÉCILE	Monsieur?
	(FEYDEAU *turns.* CÉCILE *approaches him with a determined look.*)
FEYDEAU	Where's your husband?
CÉCILE	I got rid of him.
FEYDEAU	(*ushers her back towards the hall*) Cécile, I'm sorry . . .
	(CÉCILE *kisses him passionately.* FEYDEAU *responds, helpless.*)
CÉCILE	(*breathless*) I want to see you. Tonight.
FEYDEAU	I can't.
CÉCILE	(*into his ear*) Yes, you can. I'll perform my monologue. Then we'll perform a dialogue.
CHILD	(*off*) Mama!
FEYDEAU	(*jumps back*) You must go!
CÉCILE	I need to talk to you! Please! (*Beat.*) Can't we talk at least?

FEYDEAU	(*sigh*) The Tricolour café. Two doors down. (*Checks his watch.*) I'll be there in two minutes.
	(*She kisses him and leaves. Pause. He tiptoes towards the bedroom.* YVETTE *enters.*)
FEYDEAU	Yvette! (FEYDEAU *locates his shoes and begins to put one on.*) Tell Madame I've gone out for . . . um . . .
	(MARIANNE *enters.*)
MARIANNE	Where are you going?
FEYDEAU	I need some . . . paper.
MARIANNE	Have you seen your son yet?
FEYDEAU	No. But I will.
MARIANNE	Yvette will fetch the paper.
FEYDEAU	No, it's fine.
MARIANNE	You will spend some time with your son! And Yvette will fetch the paper! That is my final word!
	(MARIANNE *returns to the bedroom.* FEYDEAU *contemplates the situation while* YVETTE *suppresses a smile.* FEYDEAU *quickly writes a note on* MARIANNE'S *rather crumpled writing paper.*)
FEYDEAU	Madame Habillot is in the Tricolour. Please deliver this to her.
	(FEYDEAU *puts the note into an envelope and hands it to* YVETTE. *She holds onto his hand.*)
YVETTE	Georges, I was thinking . . . Maybe we could meet at the Hotel some time. Like we used to . . .

(She places his hand against her breast. He withdraws it immediately.)

FEYDEAU (*sharply*) Yvette, you forget yourself! (*Beat.*) The Tricolour. Straight away.

(Beat. She curtsies with a sarcastic smile and marches towards the hall. But a thought occurs.)

YVETTE Isn't it closed?

FEYDEAU What?

YVETTE The Tricolour. For refurbishment.

FEYDEAU Well, go and find her anyway! She'll be out there somewhere!

(She exits to the hall with a sigh.)

FEYDEAU Oh, and get me some paper.

(LEVASSEUR enters from the bedroom, followed by DIDIER and MARIANNE.)

LEVASSEUR I must talk to him . . .

DIDIER Monsieur, you're in no condition . . .

MARIANNE Talk to whom?

LEVASSEUR My father. I ran straight into him! My trousers trailing!

MARIANNE Your father attacked you?!

LEVASSEUR No! No, my father is a great man!

(LEVASSEUR is unsteady – they help him into a chair.)

MARIANNE A writer?

LEVASSEUR	No. But, a man of... many talents... Now a musician. An organist.
MARIANNE	Really? In the church?
LEVASSEUR	No, in the park. His monkey attacked me.
MARIANNE	He has a monkey?
LEVASSEUR	De Sade. He's a beast! He ran off with my script! I expect he's eating it now.
DIDIER	De Sade?
FEYDEAU	The Monkey De Sade?
LEVASSEUR	My father acquired him when I was a boy. And he's terrorised me ever since! I hate him! In fact, all animals! I can't go to the circus! Or the zoo! Immediately I'm sweating, trembling...
FEYDEAU	Louis, we are all monkeys.
LEVASSEUR	I beg your pardon?!
FEYDEAU	Do you know of Charles Darwin? The English naturalist?
LEVASSEUR	Of course.
FEYDEAU	We are no longer created in the image of God. But the image of monkeys.
MARIANNE	Some more than others.
LEVASSEUR	(*impassioned*) We are not born monkeys, Monsieur; we are made monkeys!
CHILD	(*off*) Mama!
MARIANNE	(*irritated*) Georges!
FEYDEAU	I'll see what he wants.

(LEVASSEUR *stands and addresses* FEYDEAU *as the latter exits to the house.*)

LEVASSEUR My father was a craftsman! (FEYDEAU *has gone but he continues as his trousers fall to his ankles.* MARIANNE *averts her gaze.*) He made beautiful furniture! Chairs and tables! But no one wants quality any more! Everything is mass-produced! He was forced to work in the factory. As a 'leg man', if you please! Making legs only!

DIDIER Monsieur, your . . .

LEVASSEUR (*over*) For a pittance! Tragically, he took to the bottle . . . My father was an artisan! A noble craftsman! He made sacrifices for the sake of my education! And I was determined to reward him! To release him from the prison of poverty! But it is my prison too! I cannot escape!

DIDIER Monsieur, your trousers . . .

LEVASSEUR My trousers are ruined, Monsieur! And that's the end of it! This is not some stupid Feydeau farce! This is not bourgeois immorality! This is poverty! (CÉCILE *enters cautiously from the hall.*) I cannot afford trousers that last more than a month so to hell with it! (*He throws his trousers in the air.* CÉCILE *catches them with a startled expression.*) I shall live like this! I shall walk the streets of Paris! Parade my humiliation! (*He begins to parade around the room.*) Perhaps others will follow my lead! No longer sans-culotte, but sans-pantalon!

(*He parades around the room singing the Marseillaise.*)

MARIANNE Louis, calm down!

(MARIANNE *pursues him. He parades more quickly but begins to stagger.* DIDIER *is distracted by* CÉCILE.)

MARIANNE Didier, help me!

(LEVASSEUR *runs into the house, after* FEYDEAU, *singing loudly.* MARIANNE *follows.*)

MARIANNE (*off*) Didier!

CÉCILE (*aside*) At least Le Petomane was in tune.

DIDIER (*anxious*) I'm not sure what I can do . . . He seems mentally disturbed . . .

CÉCILE (*holding* LEVASSEUR'S *trousers*) Where is Monsieur Feydeau?

DIDIER Why?

CÉCILE The café is closed. (*She hands the trousers to* DIDIER.)

DIDIER Is there something I should know? About you and Georges?

CÉCILE (*angrily*) Nothing! In fact I find him thoroughly unpleasant!

DIDIER Cécile, I love you. (CÉCILE *sighs.*) I've missed you terribly.

CÉCILE (*affected by him*) I've missed you too, but . . .

DIDIER Meet me tonight. At the Hotel Terminus!

CÉCILE Why?

DIDIER I need to pick up my hat.

CÉCILE You left it?

DIDIER It was too wet to wear.

CÉCILE	Will Monsieur Feydeau be there?
DIDIER	No.
CÉCILE	How do we get in?
DIDIER	(*takes the key from his pocket*) I have his key! This is his jacket! It was in the pocket!
CÉCILE	(*takes the key*) I just gave that back to him!
HABILLOT	(*off*) Cécile?
	(DIDIER *exits to the bedroom with the trousers.* CÉCILE *returns the key to her purse.* HABILLOT *enters from the hall.*)
CÉCILE	I told you to go home.
HABILLOT	I'd rather wait. I've seen so little of you recently. Did you audition yet?
CÉCILE	Alphonse, what are you doing this evening?
HABILLOT	Why?
CÉCILE	I thought I should visit mother . . .
HABILLOT	Not tonight.
CÉCILE	She's been ill recently.
HABILLOT	She's always ill!
CÉCILE	(*little girl voice*) Alphonse . . . ?
HABILLOT	Absolutely not! How do I know you won't end up in your underwear with Monsieur Feydeau again?
CÉCILE	I was auditioning!
HABILLOT	And why did you tell him that I'm inhibited?

CÉCILE	Well, you are.
HABILLOT	(*leading her out*) Nonsense! I have no inhibitions whatsoever! And tonight I'll prove it to you!
CÉCILE	Wait a moment. I'll just say farewell to Doctor er . . . Monsieur Feydeau.
HABILLOT	Quickly.

(*She exits to the bedroom.* YVETTE *enters from the hall.*)

YVETTE	Was that your wife? I have a . . . (*She holds up* FEYDEAU'S *note but then returns it quickly to her pocket.*)
HABILLOT	Sorry?
YVETTE	Never mind. I loved your impressions, by the way.
HABILLOT	Did you?
YVETTE	Will you do the dog again?
HABILLOT	The dog?
YVETTE	A little bit! Please!
HABILLOT	Grrrrr! (YVETTE *giggles.*) Woof! Woof!
YVETTE	Brilliant! You should be on stage!
HABILLOT	You think so?
YVETTE	I bet you can act, too. And you're so tall and handsome . . .
HABILLOT	Well, coming from such a beautiful young woman . . .

(*They hold each other's gaze for a moment.* HABILLOT *begins a low growl.*)

YVETTE | Where is your wife?

HABILLOT | Er . . . She's in there. (*He indicates the bedroom.*) With Monsieur Feydeau.

YVETTE | Oh . . . ! Monsieur's bedroom? Shall I take a peek?

HABILLOT | Sorry?

YVETTE | Do you trust her?

HABILLOT | Trust her?! Oh, yes! Absolutely!

YVETTE | Monsieur Feydeau has a reputation with the ladies.

HABILLOT | Oh, I'm sure that's just gossip. Because of his plays. (*Smile.*) People must imagine he's just dramatising personal experiences!

YVETTE | I could tell you a few stories . . .

(HABILLOT'S *demeanour changes.*)

HABILLOT | My dear, you're talking about your employer. You mustn't say such things!

(YVETTE *stares, chastened.* MARIANNE *enters from the house.*)

MARIANNE | Yvette! A glass of water, please. For Monsieur Levasseur.

(*She returns to the house.* YVETTE *moves to leave but hesitates.*)

YVETTE | (*mischievous*) Oh! I nearly forgot. This is for you. From Monsieur Feydeau.

HABILLOT | Really?

YVETTE I think he said *Monsieur* Habillot.

(*She hands him* FEYDEAU'S *note for* CÉCILE, *then exits quickly to the hall.* HABILLOT *opens the envelope.*)

HABILLOT (*reads*) "I insist you pull up your stockings!" Goodness . . . (*He is baffled for a moment, then turns the page over.*) Ah! "Come to the Hotel Terminus tonight at eight o'clock. This is a private audition. Please tell no one. Not a soul. Love, Georges."

(*After a thought,* HABILLOT *celebrates silently, then swiftly selects a piece of* MARIANNE'S *crumpled writing paper.*)

HABILLOT (*speaking as he writes*) "I am delighted that you appreciate my talents. Naturally, I will be at the Hotel Terminus at eight o'clock this evening. You can count on my punctuality and my discretion." (*He hesitates.*) "Love, Alphonse."

(HABILLOT *folds up the note but then hides it in his pocket as* YVETTE *returns with a slightly concerned expression.*)

YVETTE Are you all right, Monsieur?

HABILLOT Yes! Fine! Why d'you ask?

YVETTE The note . . .

HABILLOT Oh, it was nothing! A list of . . . theatre producers.

(YVETTE *frowns, confused. Pause.*)

YVETTE (*glance at the bedroom door*) Your wife's still in there?

HABILLOT Yes. Auditioning, I imagine.

YVETTE	Well, she's very lucky. He wouldn't normally audition at home.
HABILLOT	Really? (*He hesitates.*) Where would he audition? Normally. The theatre . . . ?
YVETTE	Or the hotel.
HABILLOT	(*casual*) I see.
YVETTE	The Hotel Terminus. (*She takes the hotel key out of her pocket.*) Room one-eight-nine.
HABILLOT	You have a key?
YVETTE	There are many keys. He hands them out to his favourites.
HABILLOT	Favourite actors?
YVETTE	Perhaps you'd like to audition for me some time . . . ?

(*He stares, confused.* MARIANNE *bursts in from the house.*)

MARIANNE	Yvette! Water!
YVETTE	Oh! Beg your pardon, Madame!

(*She exits to the hall at speed.* MARIANNE *follows her muttering.*)

MARIANNE	For heaven's sake . . . If you want anything done . . . (*She stops at the door to the hall and turns to* HABILLOT.) Monsieur, aren't you a policeman? Why don't you do something?
HABILLOT	About what?
MARIANNE	The assault, of course!

(*She exits to the hall.*)

HABILLOT   What assault?!

(*He follows her.* CÉCILE *enters from the bedroom, straightening her hair. She looks around.*)

CÉCILE   Alphonse? (*Pause.*) Gone, has he? How rude. (*She wanders out to the hall. Off:*) Alphonse?

(DIDIER *enters from the bedroom, still holding* LEVASSEUR'S *trousers.* MARIANNE *enters at speed from the hall with a glass of water. She sees* DIDIER *and stops.*)

MARIANNE   Where did you disappear to?

(DIDIER *opens his mouth to speak.*)

HABILLOT   (*off, with volume*) Madame!

(MARIANNE *turns towards the hall.* DIDIER, *trousers in hand, exits swiftly to the house.* HABILLOT *enters.*)

HABILLOT   Madame, who was assaulted?

MARIANNE   Monsieur Levasseur! Outside in the street!

(CÉCILE *enters behind* HABILLOT.)

MARIANNE   Didn't you see anything? I assumed that's why you're still here.

CÉCILE   We're just leaving.

HABILLOT   Well . . .

MARIANNE   No, that's fine. I'm sure we'll cope. (*She marches towards the house.*) Where did that idiot doctor go?

(*Exit* MARIANNE.)

HABILLOT	I should make a few enquiries. (*He gestures towards the bedroom.*) Is Monsieur Feydeau . . . ?
CÉCILE	No! No, he's . . . (*Points vaguely in a different direction.*) . . . in the . . . drawing-room, I think.
HABILLOT	My darling. I've been thinking . . . Perhaps I was a bit hasty. How is your mother exactly?
CÉCILE	Oh, she'll be fine.
HABILLOT	But she's getting on. She won't be around for ever. If you want to see her this evening . . .
CÉCILE	You're the sweetest man.
HABILLOT	Wait there a moment.

(HABILLOT *exits to the house.* CÉCILE *tiptoes into the bedroom. But she returns with a frown and looks around again.*)

CÉCILE Benoit?

(*She considers her options for a moment, then quickly selects another piece of writing paper and scribbles a note.*)

CÉCILE (*under her breath*) "My dearest, try as I might, I can't resist you. For some strange reason, my heart beats more quickly when you're near. I will see you tonight at the hotel, as you suggest."

(FEYDEAU *enters from the hall.*)

FEYDEAU Ah! There you are! I escaped to look for you. Did you get . . .

(DIDIER *enters, from the house.*)

CÉCILE Sorry?

DIDIER Cécile? You're still here.

CÉCILE Yes, I was just . . . (*Pause. Glances between them.*) Anyway! I must go. My husband is waiting. (*She kisses* DIDIER *on the cheek.*) That's such a lovely jacket! (*She puts her note in* DIDIER'S *pocket under the pretence of inspecting his jacket.*)

DIDIER Thank you.

FEYDEAU It doesn't fit you.

CÉCILE Oh, I think it does.

FEYDEAU No, look. (FEYDEAU *takes the jacket from* DIDIER *and puts it on.*) There! Made to measure.

DIDIER I must get one.

CÉCILE What material is it?

(*She inspects the jacket again and tries to put her hand in* FEYDEAU'S *pocket.* (FEYDEAU *thinks she is trying to put something into his pocket.*) DIDIER *stares, frowning.*)

FEYDEAU It's . . . er . . . velvet . . . With a . . . silk lining. (FEYDEAU *puts his hands in his jacket pockets and pulls out a few items including a pen and* CÉCILE'S *note.*) I shouldn't really keep things in my pockets. It spoils the line. (*He throws the pen onto the table and puts* CÉCILE'S *note into his trouser pocket.*) How's that? (*He strikes a pose.*)

MARIANNE (*off*) Georges!

FEYDEAU Tell her you haven't seen me.

(*He exits swiftly to the hall.*)

DIDIER Why are women so damned superficial!

CÉCILE I beg your pardon?!

DIDIER First you're affectionate with me. Then he puts on the stupid jacket and you're all over him!

CÉCILE I put a note in your pocket! *His* pocket! A love note!

DIDIER A love note?

CÉCILE Well, a . . . sort of . . . It could be interpreted . . . as such. (DIDIER *stares at her, smiling slightly.*) He put it in his trousers. (*He continues staring which irritates her.*) Benoit!

DIDIER Yes?

CÉCILE We must retrieve it!

DIDIER (*boldly*) I'll just ask him! I'll say 'there's a note in your pocket intended for me'.

CÉCILE Well, quickly!

(CÉCILE *exits to the hall, followed by* DIDIER. MARIANNE *enters from the house.*)

MARIANNE (*frustrated*) Georges! Where on earth . . .

(*She exits to the bedroom as* FEYDEAU *enters tentatively from the house. Once satisfied that the coast is clear, he takes the note from his trousers.*)

FEYDEAU "My entire left cheek is throbbing . . . " (*Recognising his own writing, he quickly turns the page over. He reads* CÉCILE's *note:*) "My dearest, try as I might, I can't resist you. For some strange reason, my heart beats more quickly when you're near. I will see you tonight at the hotel, as you suggest."

(MARIANNE *enters from the bedroom with a pillow.*)

MARIANNE   Ah! How is Jacques?

FEYDEAU   Fine.

MARIANNE   'Fine'? He's not 'fine'!

(*Without breaking stride, she exits to the house.* FEYDEAU *lifts the table cloth, opens a small drawer in the table and hides the note in it. He locks the drawer and puts the tiny key in the inside pocket of his jacket* (*where it will remain until act three*). MARIANNE *enters from the house without the pillow.*)

MARIANNE   Constipation is very serious. Apparently the bastard son of Louis XV nearly died from chronic constipation at the age of seven!

(*She exits to the hall.* FEYDEAU *begins to write.*)

FEYDEAU   (*under his breath*) 'Constipation is very serious. Apparently the bastard son ... '

(MARIANNE *enters from the hall with a basket of fruit. She notices he is writing and casts a furtive glance over his shoulder.*)

MARIANNE   What are you writing now?

FEYDEAU   Nothing.

(FEYDEAU *folds up the piece of paper so she can't read it.*)

MARIANNE   (*sigh*) I'm not interested.

(*She exits to the house.* FEYDEAU *puts the paper in his trouser pocket.* DIDIER *and* CÉCILE *enter silently from the hall. They see* FEYDEAU. DIDIER *gestures urgently to* CÉCILE *to return to the hall. She does so.* DIDIER *approaches* FEYDEAU.)

DIDIER   Georges? (FEYDEAU *turns.*) I believe you have something . . .

FEYDEAU   (*searching his jacket pockets*) Where's my key?!

DIDIER   Sorry?

FEYDEAU   It was in this pocket. (FEYDEAU *stares at* DIDIER, *scrutinising.*)

DIDIER   Perhaps it fell out . . .

FEYDEAU   (*severely, sensing he is lying*) Benoit, that is my hotel room. It is for my use only.

DIDIER   Yes! Of course! I don't have the key.

FEYDEAU   But you're up to something. Clearly. There's a spring in your step.

DIDIER   (*falling to pieces*) No, I . . . Not at all. That's . . . No doubt that's just . . . trapped wind . . .

MARIANNE   (*off*) Georges!

FEYDEAU   For heaven's sake! Can't a man have some peace and quiet in his own home!

                (*He exits to the bedroom and slams the door.* DIDIER *stands, immobile, wondering what to do.* CÉCILE *enters tentatively.* DIDIER *tiptoes to the bedroom door and tries the handle.*)

DIDIER   Locked.

CÉCILE   Did you get it?

DIDIER   I may have to steal it. From his trousers.

CÉCILE   (*annoyed*) Why didn't you ask him?!

DIDIER	He's suspicious already . . .
CÉCILE	Of what?!
DIDIER	Knock on the door! Say you need to speak to him! About . . . some theatre nonsense . . .
CÉCILE	What?!
DIDIER	Distract him somehow! Do your audition! And I will pick his pocket from behind!
CÉCILE	No, I'll pick his pocket.
DIDIER	No, no, I don't want you putting your hands in Monsieur Feydeau's trousers.
CÉCILE	But you're so hopeless!
DIDIER	My dear, I have been married for fifteen years! I am a master of subterfuge!

(DIDIER *moves to knock on the bedroom door.*)

HABILLOT	(*off*) Monsieur Feydeau?
DIDIER	Quick!

(DIDIER *takes her hand and leads her out to the hall as* HABILLOT *enters from the house, followed by* MARIANNE.)

HABILLOT	I'd like a brief word.
MARIANNE	(*irritated*) I don't know where he is.
HABILLOT	Cécile? (*He looks around.*) Now my wife's gone, too.
MARIANNE	Well, that's marriage for you.
HABILLOT	She may be outside.

MARIANNE Quite possibly. Good day, Monsieur.

HABILLOT I have a note . . . For Monsieur Feydeau.

(LEVASSEUR *enters from the house. He is trouserless and eating a banana.*)

MARIANNE I will hand it to him.

HABILLOT I'd rather deliver it myself.

MARIANNE Monsieur, I will hand it to him directly.

(*Pause.* HABILLOT *hands her the note, then bows, turns on his heel and exits to the hall.*)

MARIANNE Something's going on . . . (*She opens the note and reads it.*) "Everyone in my position wears lace underwear!" Good Lord!

LEVASSEUR Doesn't surprise me at all.

MARIANNE (*turns the page over*) "I am delighted that you appreciate my talents. Naturally, I will be at the Hotel Terminus at eight o'clock this evening. You can count on my punctuality and my discretion. Love, Alphonse." (*Anger boils up.*) Swine! He's going to that wretched hotel again! (*She paces around the room, raging.*) For another of his . . . sordid assignations!

LEVASSEUR With a policeman . . . ?

MARIANNE How do I know?! A ménage a trios, perhaps!

LEVASSEUR (*disturbed*) Really?

(*She returns the note to its envelope and discards it dismissively.*)

MARIANNE He was hiding something . . . Earlier. In his pocket.

(YVETTE *enters from the hall.*)

YVETTE	(*meekly*) Madame?
MARIANNE	That blasted hotel! Lord knows what he gets up to!
YVETTE	Has Monsieur Habillot gone?
MARIANNE	Just look at his plays! They're all the same! Act one at home! The adulterous husband arranges a tryst! At a hotel!
	(YVETTE *notices the note from* HABILLOT. *She picks it up.*)
LEVASSEUR	Yes. Indeed.
MARIANNE	He lies to his wife! Invents some stupid story which falls apart! So he lies even more!
YVETTE	Madame?
MARIANNE	What?!
YVETTE	This note . . .
MARIANNE	Yes?! It's from Monsieur Habillot!
YVETTE	For me?
MARIANNE	The sordid web of deceit gets more and more tangled!
YVETTE	(*reads the note and frowns*) " . . . lace underwear"!
MARIANNE	Mistaken identities! Ridiculous misunderstandings!
YVETTE	(*turns the page over and reads quietly to herself*) " . . . delighted that your appreciate my talents."

MARIANNE	By the end of act one, everyone – for the most ABSURD, CONTRIVED reasons – plans to visit the same hotel!
YVETTE	" . . . I will be at the Hotel Terminus . . . "
MARIANNE	Including the long-suffering wife! Who plans revenge if she catches him!
LEVASSEUR	Does she?
YVETTE	"Love, Alphonse."
MARIANNE	Well, who can blame her?!
LEVASSEUR	No, indeed.
MARIANNE	At the hotel, a ludicrous farce ensues until the truth is revealed! Or, at least, half-revealed!
YVETTE	Madame . . .
MARIANNE	Stop interrupting!
	(YVETTE *curtsies and leaves to the hall with a spring in her step.*)
LEVASSEUR	Then the third act back at home. The husband has to face the music.
MARIANNE	Exactly!
LEVASSEUR	(*warming to her anger*) Who, with any theatrical experience, does not know it all by heart?
MARIANNE	He will certainly face the music!
LEVASSEUR	(*dismissive*) Vaudeville via Scribe, the 'well-made play'!
MARIANNE	And it won't be very tuneful!

LEVASSEUR	He is just following rules laid down by others! He is not an artist! Merely a craftsman!
MARIANNE	I thought you were for craftsmen.
LEVASSEUR	I am for craftsmen.
MARIANNE	In spite of craftsmen.

(LEVASSEUR *is studying, at arm's length, the pages on the table.*)

MARIANNE	That's his new play. Looks utterly frightful. You can read it if you like.
LEVASSEUR	Oh, no, I'd rather not waste precious time.

(LEVASSEUR *remains drawn to the script for the remainder of the scene.* CÉCILE *enters from the house, followed by* DIDIER.)

MARIANNE	Ah! Madame Habillot. Your husband just left.
CÉCILE	Oh . . . I see. I was looking for . . . Monsieur Feydeau.
MARIANNE	Why? Do you have a note for him?

(CÉCILE *and* DIDIER *stiffen, then glance at each other.*)

CÉCILE	No . . . It was not for him.
MARIANNE	Sorry?
CÉCILE	He had a note. Of mine. On his person. (MARIANNE *stares.*) Did he mention it?
MARIANNE	He mentioned nothing.

(FEYDEAU *enters from the bedroom.*)

FEYDEAU	What's going on?

MARIANNE	Georges! Apparently, you have a note on your person.
CÉCILE	No, no. It doesn't matter.
HABILLOT	(*off*) Cécile?
	(DIDIER *ducks under the table again.* HABILLOT *enters from the hall.*)
HABILLOT	Ah! There you are. Are we going?
FEYDEAU	Levasseur, where are your trousers?
LEVASSEUR	I've no idea.
HABILLOT	Were they stolen too?
MARIANNE	(*looking around*) Didier's disappeared again!
HABILLOT	It's appalling – they'll steal anything these days! Monsieur, I should take a description. Before I go.
LEVASSEUR	Sorry?
HABILLOT	Of your assailant. If we have any hope of arrest . . .
FEYDEAU	(*sighs, sits*) For heaven's sake . . .
LEVASSEUR	He is about . . . so high. (*He indicates roughly three feet from the ground.*) Hairy. Very long arms.
FEYDEAU	Practically a dwarf!
HABILLOT	There is no way your trousers would fit him! This was a motiveless attack!
MARIANNE	It was a monkey. Not a dwarf.
LEVASSEUR	The motive was hatred.

HABILLOT	Of your trousers?
LEVASSEUR	My trousers are irrelevant.
HABILLOT	Monsieur, I am a Police Inspector. I will decide what is relevant and what isn't.

(*The table moves slightly towards where* FEYDEAU *is sitting. Only* CÉCILE *notices. She begins shuffling unobtrusively to the other side of the room.*)

FEYDEAU	I'm afraid I need to work. So, could you all please leave?
CÉCILE	(*drawing attention away from the table*) Perhaps I could audition for you! Very quickly.
MARIANNE	Not at the moment.

(YVETTE *enters from the house with* LEVASSEUR'S *trousers.*)

YVETTE	Monsieur Levasseur, your trousers. (*She hands them to* LEVASSEUR.)
HABILLOT	A-ha!
LEVASSEUR	Thank you.
MARIANNE	I need to speak to my husband. Could everyone . . .

(*The table moves again.*)

HABILLOT	Did that table move?
CÉCILE	(*suddenly, with conviction*) "No, I'm off! It's driving me mad! Just over there, in the next room, there's that man! You know, that man who does monologues! Look, he's doing one now!"

HABILLOT	Who?! Where?!
CÉCILE	I'm performing a monologue! By Monsieur Feydeau.
HABILLOT	You said someone next door was performing a monologue.
CÉCILE	It's a monologue about monologues.

(*Surreptitiously,* LEVASSEUR *picks up a couple of pages from the table and studies them.*)

MARIANNE	This is not the time or the place.
CÉCILE	"Monologues! The very idea! If I were Prefect . . . "
HABILLOT	Monsieur Levasseur, please put on your trousers!
LEVASSEUR	(*hiding the pages*) Why?
CÉCILE	"If I were Prefect of Police, I'd ban them!"
HABILLOT	Ban trousers?! Why on earth . . . ?
CÉCILE	Alphonse! You're ruining my monologue!
HABILLOT	Monsieur Levasseur . . . !
LEVASSEUR	My trousers are torn! They do not stay up.
HABILLOT	Hold them up!

(*The table moves again.*)

CÉCILE	(*louder*) "If I were Prefect of Police, I'd ban them! They're utterly false! A reasonable man doesn't just talk out loud. He thinks, so he doesn't need to talk. That's what separates him from the idiots who speak without thinking."

(*Without looking,* LEVASSEUR *attempts to drop the paper back onto the table. But the table has moved so the paper falls onto the floor. He bends over to pick it up catching* HABILLOT'S *attention again.*)

HABILLOT (*losing his temper*) Monsieur, my wife will not perform for a man with no trousers!

MARIANNE (*aside*) That's not what I've heard.

HABILLOT If you do not put them on, I will arrest you.

FEYDEAU This is my house! You cannot arrest a man for being trouserless in a private house!

HABILLOT This is a public gathering!

FEYDEAU No, it is not! You are uninvited guests in my study! And you will arrest no one!

HABILLOT With the greatest respect, Monsieur, I can arrest who I like!

FEYDEAU Well, then, arrest me! (*He swiftly removes his trousers.*)

MARIANNE For goodness sake . . .

HABILLOT My dear, perhaps we should leave.

CÉCILE Can't I continue for a moment?

FEYDEAU If you are so prudish, Monsieur, that you can't bear a man in his underwear . . . !

HABILLOT Prudish?

FEYDEAU You will get nowhere in show business!

HABILLOT It is nothing to do with that!

FEYDEAU (*over*) You cannot afford to be prim! Or priggish! Or inhibited!

HABILLOT	Inhibited?! I am not inhibited at all! (*He swiftly removes his trousers and drops them near the table.*) There! My dear, please continue!
MARIANNE	This is absurd.
CÉCILE	"Personally, I would only allow monologues if there's more than one person. Because then it's no longer a monologue. It's two people talking to each other. And when we listen to them, we're eavesdropping. They don't bother us. But someone who just reels off a monologue in front of you . . . What right does he have! Who asked him to?" (DIDIER's *hand emerges and begins to pull* HABILLOT's *trousers under the table.*) "What if I walked up to you and started reciting one? Well, what would you say? It's false! Utterly false! Isn't it? Good. We're agreed."

(HABILLOT *notices that his trousers are disappearing.*)

HABILLOT	The monkey! The trouser thief! He's under the table! (*The trousers disappear.*) Ssshh! (HABILLOT *drops silently to his knees and approaches the table slowly on all fours, backside in the air.*) Softly, softly . . .
FEYDEAU	What a privilege to watch a professional at work.
HABILLOT	Ssshh!

(HABILLOT *lifts the table cloth slowly.* DIDIER *appears from the other side and, clutching* HABILLOT's *trousers, runs out of the room.*)

HABILLOT	Where did he go? (FEYDEAU *points.*) Was it a monkey?

FEYDEAU	Well . . . barely human. (FEYDEAU *picks up his own trousers.*)
MARIANNE	It was the idiot doctor.
	(HABILLOT *runs out in pursuit of* DIDIER *but returns directly.*)
HABILLOT	I cannot leave the house like this!
FEYDEAU	No. Indeed.
HABILLOT	Your trousers, Monsieur.
FEYDEAU	Sorry?
HABILLOT	I will have to commandeer your trousers.
FEYDEAU	On what authority?
HABILLOT	My own authority.
FEYDEAU	You cannot commandeer a man's trousers.
HABILLOT	If necessary, Monsieur, I can have your trousers subpoenaed.
FEYDEAU	Nonsense! (HABILLOT *snatches for* FEYDEAU'S *trousers. A tug of war ensues.*) Get off! For God's sake, man!
HABILLOT	(*over*) Let go!
YVETTE	(*over, trying to release* HABILLOT'S *hands*) You'll tear Monsieur's trousers!
	(MARIANNE *takes the opportunity to rifle through* FEYDEAU'S *jacket pockets from behind.* CÉCILE *tries to reach into one of* FEYDEAU'S *trouser pockets.* LEVASSEUR *assists* YVETTE *in her efforts to stop the tug of war.*)
FEYDEAU	Get off! Let go!

HABILLOT	(*over*) Desist, Monsieur! I need your trousers!
YVETTE	(*over*) Stop it! Both of you!

(CÉCILE *retrieves the note from the trouser pocket.* FEYDEAU *is distracted by this.*)

FEYDEAU What are you doing?!

(CÉCILE *runs out to the hall.* HABILLOT *wins the tug of war and follows her, clutching* FEYDEAU'S *trousers.* FEYDEAU *pursues him, followed by* YVETTE.)

FEYDEAU Stop! You thief!

(MARIANNE *pursues them, followed by* LEVASSEUR, *who is trying to put on his trousers.*)

MARIANNE My life is an utter farce!

(*A moment later,* LEVASSEUR *returns and steals the pages from the table. He then runs after the others, his trousers falling.*)

(*No interval. The third movement of the Ravel Violin Sonata is played loudly as the stage is transformed swiftly from* FEYDEAU'S *study into* FEYDEAU'S *room at the Hotel Terminus.*)

ACT TWO

Dingy hotel room. Large bed. Three exits. Doors leading to the hotel, an adjoining room and a bathroom. In the fourth corner of the stage stands a wardrobe.

There is also a chest of drawers, a small table and a bedside table. Many books are in evidence as well as glasses, cups, several bottles of perfume and the remnants of a sandwich. DIDIER'S *top hat stands on the small table. There is much clutter but a strong sense of order.*

FEYDEAU *enters in his underwear, smoking his pipe. He walks over to the wardrobe and returns with a pair of trousers which he inspects, then hangs over the back of a chair. He then returns to the bathroom, closing the door behind him.*

MARIANNE *and* LEVASSEUR *enter from the hotel.* LEVASSEUR, *clearly anxious, clutches a walking stick.*

MARIANNE	Here we are. Dingy hotel room. Large bed. Clearly, act two.
	(MARIANNE *proceeds to inspect the room.*)
LEVASSEUR	The door was unlocked. Does that mean there's someone in here?
MARIANNE	Not necessarily.
LEVASSEUR	I hate hotels. Bourgeois dens of debauchery.
MARIANNE	Louis, if all you know of society is from watching my husband's plays, then you know very little indeed!
LEVASSEUR	Did you say you've read his new one?
MARIANNE	No. Just a page or so.
LEVASSEUR	I was rather shocked. Some of the ideas I discussed with him in the past . . . For my own plays . . .

MARIANNE	He stole them?
LEVASSEUR	Stole them and . . . perverted them. Also . . . (*He hesitates.*) The wife character. Is rather surprising.
MARIANNE	A complete harridan?
LEVASSEUR	You could say that.

(*She inspects the remnants of* FEYDEAU'S *food.*)

MARIANNE	Food for one . . . Or two?

(MARIANNE *throws salt over her left shoulder, narrowly missing* LEVASSEUR.)

LEVASSEUR	Careful!
MARIANNE	Sorry! It was salt. I'm afraid I'm rather superstitious.

(*Noises off.* MARIANNE *listens at the bathroom door. More noises.*)

MARIANNE	(*indicates the door to the adjoining room*) Quick! Through here!
LEVASSEUR	(*distressed*) No, I'll wait downstairs.

(LEVASSEUR *exits to the hotel.*)

MARIANNE	I need a witness!

(MARIANNE *exits to the adjoining room as* FEYDEAU *enters from the bathroom. His chin is covered in shaving foam. He looks around suspiciously then opens the door to the hotel and peers out. Seeing no one, he closes the door, locks it and places the key on top of the chest of drawers. He then returns to the bathroom. A moment later, the door to the hotel is unlocked from the outside and* DIDIER, *carrying a doctor's bag, enters cautiously, followed by* CÉCILE. DIDIER *locks the door behind them.*)

DIDIER A-ha! (*He inspects his hat.*) Dry as a bone! (DIDIER *returns it to the table and places the key next to it.*)

CÉCILE How could you steal the wrong trousers? How could you be so stupid? (DIDIER *takes* HABILLOT's *trousers out of his bag.*) Look! They're enormous!

DIDIER You can return them. (*He hands them to her. She chucks them over the chair, on top of* FEYDEAU'S.) So, where is it? Your little love note.

CÉCILE (*searching her purse*) Don't get your hopes up. It's very brief. (*She can't find it.*) Where on earth . . . ?

DIDIER Just tell me what it said.

CÉCILE Nothing! 'See you at the Hotel.'

DIDIER You said it was a love note.

CÉCILE Yes, just a few words about how your presence affects me. Physically. (*She finds it.*) Ah!

DIDIER A-ha! (*He takes it, reads:*) "Constipation is very serious."

CÉCILE What?!

DIDIER "Apparently the bastard son of Louis XV nearly died from chronic constipation at the age of seven!"

CÉCILE That's not my note! (*She takes it and studies both sides.*)

DIDIER	You stole the wrong note?! How could you be so stupid?!
CÉCILE	(*returns the note to her purse*) Where's my note? Maybe Monsieur Feydeau has it . . .
DIDIER	Exactly! He could turn up here any moment! Thinking you want to spend the night in his hotel room!
CÉCILE	My husband ran off with Feydeau's trousers . . .
DIDIER	Well, that's worse! Your husband could turn up!
CÉCILE	Maybe it fell out in the street. Half of Paris may think I want to spend the night with them!
DIDIER	(*aside*) The other half already have.
CÉCILE	We mustn't stay too long.
	(*She grabs him and kisses him. He responds awkwardly.*)
CÉCILE	(*breathless*) Benoit . . . What is it about you . . . ?
DIDIER	I've no idea.
	(*He removes his trousers swiftly and throws them over the others. She kicks off her shoes, unfastens her dress and pulls him onto the bed.*)
CÉCILE	Neither have I.
	(*More kissing. Then he checks his pocket watch.*)
CÉCILE	Are you timing yourself?!
DIDIER	(*anxious*) What if your husband arrived . . . ? And found us here . . . ?

CÉCILE	Well, he wouldn't be pleased. (*She stretches out on the bed.*) A bit of danger . . . Always rather exciting . . .
DIDIER	Not to me. In fact, personally, I find safety exciting.
CÉCILE	Come here.
DIDIER	Is he . . . stable? Mentally.
CÉCILE	What d'you mean?
DIDIER	Are you aware of Doctor Freud from Vienna?
CÉCILE	Who?
DIDIER	He believes that civilisation necessitates the repression of base instincts.
CÉCILE	What base instincts?
DIDIER	The beast. The animal. In all of us.
CÉCILE	What sort of doctor . . . ?
DIDIER	He's a doctor of the mind.
CÉCILE	How absurd.
DIDIER	Yes, perhaps it is. Your husband's not an animal, is he?
CÉCILE	He's a policeman!
DIDIER	(*beat*) Is that yes or no?
CÉCILE	Make love to me! Like a man!
DIDIER	I must talk to your husband! Like a man!
	(*Noise off.* DIDIER *listens at the bathroom door.*)

DIDIER	There's someone in the bathroom!
CÉCILE	What?
DIDIER	Perhaps your husband!
CÉCILE	For goodness sake . . . !
DIDIER	Ssshh!

(*Noises off.* DIDIER *picks up his bag and hides in the wardrobe.*)

CÉCILE Benoit!

(*The bathroom door opens.* CÉCILE *hides under the bed.* FEYDEAU *enters, frowning, and looks around. He has washed off the shaving foam but is still wearing underwear only. He collects his key from the top of the chest of drawers, unlocks the door to the hotel and peers out once more. He closes the door without locking it, returns the key to the chest of drawers and continues preening himself. He contemplates his perfumes and chooses the largest bottle. It is almost the size of a decanter.* MARIANNE *bursts into the room.*)

MARIANNE	Am I interrupting something?
FEYDEAU	(*holding the bottle*) Not at all.
MARIANNE	Entertaining?
FEYDEAU	What?
MARIANNE	All that perfume. You've enough there for . . . an army!
FEYDEAU	An *army*?
MARIANNE	You're clearly very keen to impress someone . . .

FEYDEAU	Actually, you're right. It's army surplus. The French army is not the fiercest in the world. But it's certainly the most fragrant.
MARIANNE	Where is she?
FEYDEAU	Who?
MARIANNE	(*mocking*) "So young, so intelligent, so beautiful . . . !" I don't think she's intelligent at all. Or beautiful. (*She stares at him for his reaction.*)
FEYDEAU	She was acting. It was an audition.
MARIANNE	What?
FEYDEAU	A Man Condemned to Death. (*He opens a drawer in which there are many scripts.*) Don't you know my work at all?
MARIANNE	What d'you want with all those? Do you take them to bed with you?
FEYDEAU	(*reads*) "I am condemned to death. At my age! So young, so intelligent, so beautiful."
MARIANNE	I thought she was lamenting her marriage to the pig farmer. Do you intend to hire her?
FEYDEAU	(*defiant*) I'm not sure.
MARIANNE	She has no talent. She can't do comedy at all.
FEYDEAU	You don't 'do' comedy. You 'do' reality. It's only funny if it's deadly serious.
MARIANNE	Anyway, she's a whore. It's well-known.

(*A gasp from under the bed. They both seem startled.* MARIANNE *looks around the room, unable to pinpoint the source of the noise.* FEYDEAU *registers this and looks around also.*)

FEYDEAU	Hotels . . . You always hear voices.
MARIANNE	(*marching around the room*) She is a whore! (*Silence.*) A harlot! (*Silence. She strides into the bathroom as* CÉCILE *emerges, seething.*) Slattern!
CÉCILE	You . . . !

(FEYDEAU *places his hand over her mouth and bundles her towards the door to the hotel.*)

MARIANNE	(*off*) Strumpet! (*Beat.*) Demi-mondaine!

(FEYDEAU *propels* CÉCILE *out of the door.*)

CÉCILE	My shoes!

(*He closes the door on her as* MARIANNE *returns.*)

MARIANNE	What was that?!
FEYDEAU	No. Nothing. Must be next door.

(MARIANNE *exits swiftly to the hotel.* FEYDEAU *kicks one of* CÉCILE'S *shoes under the bed.* MARIANNE *returns.*)

MARIANNE	What's going on?! Why did you come here tonight?
FEYDEAU	I was tired. I wanted a nap. Without interruption. Which is almost impossible at home.
MARIANNE	A nap?!
FEYDEAU	Yes! I wanted to sleep! That's what hotels are for!
MARIANNE	Really? (*She opens his drawer of plays.*) Well, perhaps you can tell me in which of your plays

	a married man goes to a hotel! And sleeps! All through act two!
FEYDEAU	Hardly the stuff of farce ...
MARIANNE	(*flicks through a script*) No, not that one. (*She throws it in his direction.*) Maybe this one! (*She glances at another then throws it over her shoulder.* FEYDEAU *tries to catch it.*) This one perhaps!
FEYDEAU	All right, stop!
	(*She takes a handful of scripts and hurls them in his general direction.*)
MARIANNE	Maybe this one! Or this one!
FEYDEAU	(*angered*) Enough!
MARIANNE	Why don't you just move in here?! Permanently! You clearly prefer it!
FEYDEAU	Well, it's certainly more peaceful! And the service is better!
MARIANNE	Oh, is that what I am to you?! Room service?!
FEYDEAU	No, I don't regard you that highly!
MARIANNE	That's it! You just want room service! You don't want a wife at all!
	(*She storms out to the hotel.*)
FEYDEAU	(*to himself*) No, I always want a wife. But never my own.
	(*After a pause for contemplation,* FEYDEAU *opens the door to the hotel and peers out.*)
FEYDEAU	(*whisper*) Cécile?

	(*No response. He looks down at his clothing – underwear only. He closes the door and hurries to the wardrobe. He opens it and discovers* DIDIER *inside. Pause.*)
DIDIER	Good evening.
	(*Pause.*)
FEYDEAU	What are you doing in there?
DIDIER	I apologise sincerely. But it's hopeless. I love her.
	(DIDIER *enters sheepishly, holding his bag. He is still without trousers.*)
FEYDEAU	Who?
DIDIER	Cécile. I brought her here.
FEYDEAU	(*confused*) You brought Cécile here?
DIDIER	All this deception will end. I've decided to confront Habillot.
FEYDEAU	He'll murder you. He's a madman.
DIDIER	Please don't say that!
FEYDEAU	(*sigh*) Benoit, I'm bored with you.
DIDIER	(*noticing his hat*) Actually, it wasn't just Cécile. I also came to collect my hat.
FEYDEAU	Did you indeed?! Well, here it is! (*Forces it onto his head.*) Now get out!
	(FEYDEAU *manhandles him out into the hotel.*)
DIDIER	Georges! Please!

(FEYDEAU *slams the door on him. A pause. He contemplates the scripts on the floor, where they will remain for the duration of the scene.*)

FEYDEAU My life's work...

(*From a drawer filled with clothes, he takes a portrait of* MARIANNE *and their children. He gazes at it. A tentative knock at the door.*)

FEYDEAU Go away!

CÉCILE (*off*) Monsieur Feydeau?

(*He opens the door.* CÉCILE *enters.*)

CÉCILE I'm terribly sorry. My shoes...

FEYDEAU Under the bed. Where's Benoit?

CÉCILE (*retrieving her shoes*) He's not here?

FEYDEAU You have to leave.

(FEYDEAU *gazes out into the hotel as* CÉCILE, *despondent, puts on her shoes.* FEYDEAU *closes and locks the door.*)

FEYDEAU Grosjean's out there.

CÉCILE Who?

FEYDEAU (*takes a dressing-gown from the wardrobe and puts it on*) The hotel manager. Perhaps the noise... someone may have complained again.

CÉCILE (*re: the portrait*) Is that your family?

FEYDEAU (*preoccupied*) Yes.

CÉCILE Beautiful children.

(*He takes the picture from her and studies it.*)

FEYDEAU	The joys of family are so delicate . . . that one must live alone to fully appreciate them.

(*Pause.*)

CÉCILE	My husband wants to take me away. Tomorrow morning. A second honeymoon. Wipe the slate clean.
FEYDEAU	Good idea.
CÉCILE	But I need to be available. To audition for you.
FEYDEAU	Not imminently.
CÉCILE	What about the Game Hunter revival?
FEYDEAU	No, that's very unlikely. You need to leave. You shouldn't be here.
CÉCILE	I'm sorry. It's Didier's fault. He persuaded me to come.
FEYDEAU	Didn't you get my note?
CÉCILE	What note?
FEYDEAU	(*beat*) Nothing. Just . . . A suggestion. For a different monologue.
CÉCILE	Oh! I have it here! (*She takes the note from her purse.*) "Constipation is very serious."
FEYDEAU	Ah! No, no. (*He takes it from her.*) That's dialogue. For a new play.
CÉCILE	Oh, is that the one you mentioned?
FEYDEAU	Sorry?
CÉCILE	You said you had a part for me.
FEYDEAU	Did I?

CÉCILE	Last night! You said you had me in mind for something.
FEYDEAU	Well, not this one. Possibly . . . a future project . . .
CÉCILE	(*slightly desperate*) If it's about constipation, look no further!
FEYDEAU	You must leave.
CÉCILE	I've had all kinds of stomach trouble!

(*A tap at the door.*)

DIDIER	(*off*) Georges! Quick!
FEYDEAU	(*to* DIDIER) Go away!
CÉCILE	You should let him in.
FEYDEAU	What if Grosjean sees me allowing a trouserless man into my room? (*A louder knock at the door.*) I'll be barred from the hotel!

(*Another knock.*)

FEYDEAU	For heaven's sake . . . ! (*He unlocks and opens the door.*) Monsieur Habillot!

(CÉCILE *scurries into the bathroom.* FEYDEAU *ensures she is out of sight before allowing* HABILLOT *into the room.*)

HABILLOT	I just saw a trouserless figure scuttling off down the corridor.
FEYDEAU	Really? Was it human?

(FEYDEAU *locks the door and puts the key in the pocket of his dressing gown.*)

HABILLOT	I think it may have been your impresario friend.

FEYDEAU	Yes, he's . . . auditioning here this evening.
HABILLOT	Without trousers?
FEYDEAU	If the audition demands it.
HABILLOT	Verisimilitude?
FEYDEAU	Exactly.
HABILLOT	Speaking of trousers . . . !
	(*He hands* FEYDEAU *a package which he opens.*)
FEYDEAU	Ah! I'll leave them out, in case they're subpoenaed.
	(*He throws his trousers on top of the others.*)
HABILLOT	I did, in fact, apprehend a suspect outside your house.
FEYDEAU	Oh, really?
HABILLOT	Decidedly not human.
FEYDEAU	The Monkey De Sade?
HABILLOT	I can't say the interrogation was very fruitful . . . (*Grin.*) But I have expanded my repertoire of animal impressions!
FEYDEAU	Excellent.
HABILLOT	Will your friend be joining us?
FEYDEAU	Sorry?
HABILLOT	For my audition. (*Knock at the door.*) Is that him?
FEYDEAU	Possibly . . . Could you wait next door for a moment? (*He indicates the adjoining room.*)

HABILLOT	Of course. (*Smile.*) I'll limber up.
FEYDEAU	Yes. Limber at will.

(HABILLOT *exits to the adjoining room.* FEYDEAU *returns to the main door, beginning to panic.*)

FEYDEAU	(*whisper*) Benoit?

(*A key is turned in the lock. This startles* FEYDEAU. *He scuttles into the bathroom.* YVETTE *enters tentatively. She hears a strange animal noise emanating from the adjoining room. She investigates.*)

YVETTE	(*off*) Oh! Alphonse!

(*The bathroom door opens.* FEYDEAU *peeks out.*)

FEYDEAU	Come on! Quick!

(FEYDEAU *leads* CÉCILE *into the room. They exit to the hotel as* YVETTE *leads* HABILLOT *by the hand into the room.*)

YVETTE	What were you doing in there?
HABILLOT	(*confused*) Just . . . limbering up . . .
YVETTE	Goodness! I'm honoured!
HABILLOT	Where is Monsieur Feydeau?
YVETTE	How should I know? At home I expect. (*She sits on the bed.*) All right, first I'd like a bit of growling.
HABILLOT	(*bewildered*) Sorry?
YVETTE	(*beat*) The dog! The growling dog!

HABILLOT	Oh. I assumed that . . . um . . . Monsieur . . .
YVETTE	Please! Just a little!

(*Pause.* HABILLOT *begins to growl. She pulls him onto the bed and kisses him.* HABILLOT *responds in spite of himself.*)

YVETTE	Keep growling.

(HABILLOT *complies but, a few moments later, extricates himself from her clutches.*)

HABILLOT	Is this Monsieur Feydeau's bed?
YVETTE	No. It's the hotel's bed.
HABILLOT	All the same . . . (*He looks around anxiously.*)
YVETTE	Would you prefer next door? The sofa?
HABILLOT	Um . . .

(YVETTE *rolls off the bed and crawls on all fours over to the adjoining room. She stops in the doorway, swaying her hips and growling provocatively.* HABILLOT, *despite himself, descends onto all fours and growls impressively. He then begins stalking her. She giggles and crawls at high speed into the adjoining room. He chases her barking into the room and slams the door behind him with a back leg.* MARIANNE *and* LEVASSEUR, *still clutching his walking stick, enter from the hotel.*)

MARIANNE	Gone. Like a thief in the night. (*She begins to investigate the room.*) I need evidence . . .

(LEVASSEUR *lowers himself into a chair. He stares at his hand which is trembling slightly.*)

MARIANNE	Louis, what on earth is the matter with you?

LEVASSEUR	I can't talk about it.
MARIANNE	Suit yourself.
LEVASSEUR	Well, if I must. I went home. This afternoon. To retrieve my play. But the beast wouldn't let me in.
MARIANNE	The Monkey De Sade?
LEVASSEUR	Father says he's protective at the moment. Because his mate has given birth. They're all living there! With my parents! Two monkeys and their baby! It's like a zoo!
MARIANNE	(*grimace*) How disgusting.
LEVASSEUR	I am such a disappointment to my father that De Sade is becoming his son and heir! He told me to my face that the baby monkey was the grandson he'd always wanted!
MARIANNE	(*moving towards the adjoining room*) What does that make you? The monkey's uncle?
LEVASSEUR	Certainly not!
MARIANNE	Ssshh!

(MARIANNE *listens at the door. Faint sounds of love-making are heard.*)

MARIANNE	He's in there! With that tart! The absolute nerve . . . ! Come here! Listen! You're my witness!
LEVASSEUR	I'd rather not.

(*She paces the room, livid, raging.*)

MARIANNE	Can you believe that man?! We have a blazing row and five minutes later he's dismissed me from his thoughts! If only that idiot policeman was here! Then there'd be trouble!

LEVASSEUR	Should we try to find him?
MARIANNE	Yes! Not just him! Any policeman! EVERY policeman! (*Opens the door to the hotel.*) Guard that door!
LEVASSEUR	Do I have to?

(MARIANNE *has gone. Despite his better judgement,* LEVASSEUR *tiptoes over to the door and listens. Barking is heard from the adjoining room.*)

LEVASSEUR	(*aghast*) Good God . . .

(*He staggers away, breathing heavily. He sees the large perfume bottle and, thinking it is a decanter, pours some of its contents into a glass and gulps it down. After a brief pause, he is choking, screaming silently.* MARIANNE *returns.*)

MARIANNE	(*anxious*) I'm not sure I want scandal. Society forgives everything, except scandal. (*She notices the key on the table.*) A-ha! (*She silently locks the door to the adjoining room.*) There! Imprisoned in his own depravity! (*She marches over to the door to the hotel and locks that also. She then returns the key to the table.*) They should all be imprisoned! All the adulterers! Removed from society!

(*Suddenly she kisses* LEVASSEUR *hard on the lips.*)

MARIANNE	Your breath is so sweet! (*They kiss passionately. His trousers fall off.*) Oh, Louis!
LEVASSEUR	My trousers are beyond my control.

(*She removes his trousers and hurls them over the others.*)

MARIANNE	(*commanding*) Get into my husband's bed!
	(*She switches off a light and strides into the bathroom. The room is dimly illuminated. After a brief hesitation,* LEVASSEUR *removes some clothing and gets into bed with his walking stick. The door to the adjoining room is unlocked and opened.* YVETTE *creeps into the room, closing the door behind her.*)
YVETTE	(*quietly*) Hello?
	(LEVASSEUR *pulls the covers up to his nose.* YVETTE, *with clothing unbuttoned, approaches the bed and reaches out hesitantly. She touches one of* LEVASSEUR'S *feet and jumps.*)
YVETTE	Oh! I'm sorry!
LEVASSEUR	(*sharply*) Who is it?
YVETTE	No one! (*Begins to button herself up. Disguising her voice:*) Just . . . room service. Do you desire anything, Monsieur Feydeau?
LEVASSEUR	(*shouting as a whisper*) Certainly not! Get out! (YVETTE *dithers.*) OUT!
	(YVETTE *curtsies habitually and runs to the hotel door. It is locked. She unlocks it with her key and leaves swiftly.*)
LEVASSEUR	'Do I desire anything?' What sort of establishment . . .
	(HABILLOT *peers into the darkened room.*)
HABILLOT	(*soft, seductive*) Coming. Ready or not.
	(LEVASSEUR *pulls the covers over his head.* HABILLOT *removes his trousers and drapes them over the others. He descends onto all fours and begins to growl as he crawls towards the bed. He lifts the bed covers, growling.*

	LEVASSEUR *is frozen, immobile.* HABILLOT *barks loudly.* LEVASSEUR *leaps out of bed, brandishing his stick and switches the light on.)*
LEVASSEUR	*(frantic)* Where is he?
HABILLOT	Who?
LEVASSEUR	There's a mangy old dog in here!
HABILLOT	Monsieur, that's the finest compliment you could possibly pay me.
	(LEVASSEUR *exits to the hotel without collecting his trousers. Rather bewildered,* HABILLOT *looks out into the hotel and then returns. He walks over to the bathroom door and knocks tentatively.)*
MARIANNE	*(off, muffled)* Just a moment.
	(HABILLOT *hesitates then switches off the light and sits in a chair, facing away from the bed and bathroom. He picks up a script from the floor and flicks through it.* MARIANNE *enters silently from the bathroom in her underwear. She sees the back of* HABILLOT'S *head, in half-light, and believes it is* LEVASSEUR. *She pulls up a stocking which has fallen and lowers herself gracefully onto the bed. She arranges herself into a variety of seductive poses and settles on one.)*
MARIANNE	*(husky voice)* Monsieur?
	(LEVASSEUR, *stick in hand, bursts in from the hotel and runs through into the bathroom, slamming the door behind him.* MARIANNE *lies still, startled. After a pause,* HABILLOT *slowly turns.* MARIANNE *rolls clumsily off the bed, crawls over to the wardrobe and clambers in. Assuming the woman is* YVETTE, HABILLOT *smiles, drops onto all fours and crawls*

towards the wardrobe, growling. He scratches at the wardrobe door and barks. YVETTE *and* FEYDEAU *enter from the hotel.* FEYDEAU *switches on the light.* HABILLOT, *on all fours, stares up at them. They stare back.*)

HABILLOT (*rising*) I'll practice next door.

FEYDEAU Good idea.

(HABILLOT *exits to the adjoining room.* FEYDEAU *locks the door to the hotel.*)

FEYDEAU Why didn't you give my note to Madame Habillot?

YVETTE I thought you said Monsieur Habillot.

FEYDEAU Nonsense.

(*An urgent knock at the door.*)

DIDIER (*off*) George! Quick! Let me in!

(FEYDEAU *sighs and unlocks the door. An exhausted and distressed* DIDIER *enters, still trouserless, hat still jammed onto his head.*)

DIDIER We're in trouble! I think he called the police!

FEYDEAU Who did?

DIDIER The hotel manager. He's been chasing me.

FEYDEAU What?

DIDIER (*racing*) Right up to floor fourteen and right back down again! On floor nine, I ran headlong into a wedding party! In my underwear! The bride screamed like a sow in labour! It echoed right down the corridor! Doors opened! Lots of little heads appeared! The hotel manager said it sounded like I assaulted her! But I barely touched her! I think she must have been anxious about the prospect of seeing her own husband in his underwear.

FEYDEAU For heaven's sake! This is a respectable establishment.

(CÉCILE *enters from the hotel.*)

CÉCILE (*to* DIDIER) There are people outside. I think they're police.

FEYDEAU There's a policeman in there as well! (*Indicates the adjoining room.*) We're surrounded.

CÉCILE What d'you mean?

FEYDEAU Your husband.

DIDIER Habillot's in there?!

FEYDEAU You need to leave!

DIDIER We cannot leave! Clearly!

FEYDEAU My reputation is at stake!

DIDIER What reputation?!

FEYDEAU Will you get out?!

(*The door to the adjoining room opens slightly.*)

HABILLOT (*off*) Monsieur Feydeau?

(FEYDEAU *blocks* HABILLOT'S *entry.*)

FEYDEAU One moment, please!

(*He closes the door.* DIDIER *tries to exit to the bathroom but the door is locked.*)

DIDIER (*whisper*) Is there someone in here?!

FEYDEAU	Just get out! This is my room!
DIDIER	Cécile, you must hide!
FEYDEAU	No! She must not!
DIDIER	In the wardrobe!
FEYDEAU	I am Georges Feydeau! Légion d'Honneur! I will not have a young woman hiding in my wardrobe! (DIDIER *opens the wardrobe.*) Besides, my wife is in there already.

(MARIANNE *enters in her underwear. She stands and returns their stares with as much defiance as she can muster.*)

MARIANNE	Can I help you?
DIDIER	Madame Feydeau. Delighted. (*He kisses her hand.*)
MARIANNE	Monsieur Didier.
CÉCILE	Madame Feydeau. (*She offers her hand.*)
MARIANNE	Mademoiselle Salvigne. (*Takes her hand.*)
CÉCILE	Madame Habillot.
MARIANNE	Madame Habillot. I beg your pardon.
FEYDEAU	Ah, to hell with the lot of you!

(*He leaves to the hotel. Beat. A knock at the door to the adjoining room.*)

HABILLOT	(*off*) Monsieur Feydeau?

(CÉCILE *moves towards the wardrobe but* MARIANNE *grabs her arm.*)

MARIANNE	That's taken.

(MARIANNE *disappears into the wardrobe.* YVETTE *hides under the bed.* CÉCILE *crawls under the bed from the other side.* DIDIER *tries to do likewise.*)

CÉCILE   Benoit! There's no room!

HABILLOT   (*off*) Monsieur?

DIDIER   (*panicking*) Just a moment!

(DIDIER *looks around for a hiding place but stops suddenly, struck by a revelation.*)

DIDIER   Madness! I must confront him, finally! Sanity must be restored!

(*He straightens his tie and repositions his hat. He stands, upright, courageous. Suddenly he realises he is not wearing trousers.*)

DIDIER   Trousers!

(*He takes* HABILLOT'S *trousers from the back of the chair and tries to put them on at great speed. He falls over. He realises they are not his, throws them across the room and inspects the next pair. Frantically, he begins throwing trousers over his head, searching for his own.*)

DIDIER   What on earth . . . !

(*The door to the adjoining room opens.* DIDIER *pulls on a pair of* HABILLOT'S *trousers and takes a deep breath.* HABILLOT *enters. A pause. They assess each other.* DIDIER *summons up some courage.*)

DIDIER   Monsieur, I respect you too much. I will not waste time with pleasantries.

HABILLOT   Very well.

(HABILLOT *launches into an extravagant monkey impression.* DIDIER *watches, shocked into immobility. Slowly, his mouth falls open. Soon* LEVASSEUR *bursts in from the bathroom with mad eyes, brandishing his stick.*)

LEVASSEUR De Sade! Where are you?!

(LEVASSEUR *searches the room frenetically. He opens the wardrobe.*)

LEVASSEUR Where is he?! The little monster!

MARIANNE (*emerging nervously*) What's the matter?

(LEVASSEUR *thrusts his stick under the bed.*)

YVETTE Ow! Careful!

(YVETTE *emerges, followed by* CÉCILE.)

HABILLOT Cécile!

(CÉCILE *runs into the bathroom.* HABILLOT *pursues her.* DIDIER *follows, fearing* HABILLOT *is dangerous.*)

DIDIER Monsieur! Stop!

LEVASSEUR Come here! You wretched animal!

(LEVASSEUR *exits to the adjoining room.* CÉCILE *returns, pursued by* HABILLOT. DIDIER, *trousers trailing, tackles* HABILLOT *around the waist.*)

DIDIER Stop him! He's a madman!

(LEVASSEUR *returns to the room.* MARIANNE *attempts to take away his stick.*)

MARIANNE Louis! Calm down!

(*A scuffle develops between* HABILLOT *and* DIDIER. YVETTE *tries to pull them apart.* FEYDEAU *enters. Simultaneous dialogue:*)

HABILLOT   Get off me! What are you doing?!

DIDIER   Help! He's a lunatic!

CÉCILE   Benoit! Alphonse! Please stop!

YVETTE   Stop it! Both of you!

LEVASSEUR   Get your hands off!

MARIANNE   Louis, calm down!

FEYDEAU   OUT!

(YVETTE *exits to the hotel, followed by* LEVASSEUR.)

LEVASSEUR   (*as he goes*) I'll find him! The dirty little beast!

MARIANNE   (*as she goes*) Louis! You're delirious!

(CÉCILE *runs out of the door followed by* HABILLOT *and* DIDIER.)

HABILLOT   (*as he goes*) Cécile!

DIDIER   (*as he goes*) I can help you! I'm a doctor!

(FEYDEAU *slams the door. The end of Ravel's Violin Sonata ('Perpetuum Mobile') builds in volume as* FEYDEAU *removes his dressing-gown and begins collecting his scripts from the floor. As the movement reaches its climax,* FEYDEAU, *cradling his scripts, gets into bed and pulls the covers over his head. Blackout. Interval.*)

ACT THREE

The next day (but a century later). London. Evening. GEORGE'S *study. The room is similar to that of Act One. The three exits lead to a bathroom, the hall and the rest of the house.*

We hear the beginning of the third movement of the Ravel Violin Sonata. GEORGE (FEYDEAU *in acts one and two) is sitting at the same table as in act one, although the table has no table cloth. He is wearing the same velvet smoking jacket and* LEVASSEUR'S *trousers. He is writing longhand on loose leaf paper. The table is covered in papers, cups etc. There is a cashmere cardigan hanging over the back of a chair.* GEORGE *takes a white handkerchief from his jacket pocket and wipes his brow.*

Doorbell. GEORGE *continues writing. Doorbell again.* GEORGE *sighs and searches through paperwork. Finally, he finds a remote control and switches off the music.*

GEORGE   Yvette!

                (Pause. YVETTE *wanders in from the house, eating an apple. She is wearing jeans and T-shirt. She stares at him vacantly.)*

GEORGE   Doorbell. (*She stares.*) Sonnette. (*Beat.*) Bell.

                (She continues staring for a moment, then wanders out to the hall. He sighs and turns the music back on. He then gets up and examines his trousers. He takes a few deliberate steps and his trousers fall down. He pulls them up and tries again. DAVID (LEVASSEUR *in acts one and two) appears in the doorway to the hall and watches.* DAVID *is wearing casual but well-fitting clothes and is somehow better-looking than* LEVASSEUR. *But he is clearly tense, preoccupied.)*

GEORGE   (*quickly, under his breath*) "My name will be enshrined for posterity whereas yours, Georges Feydeau, will be entirely forgotten!"

(*He turns to walk away and sees* DAVID. *He pulls up his trousers as they fall.*)

GEORGE   Oh, hi. Didn't see you there. (*He sits down and writes something.*) How are you?

DAVID   Fine.

(*Pause.* GEORGE *stares at* DAVID, *wondering what he wants.*)

DAVID   (*deadpan*) Congratulations. On your show.

GEORGE   Oh, you saw it?

DAVID   Yes. Um ... No. I saw a trailer, but ... Looks good. For a sitcom. But I missed the actual ... I tend to be out Monday nights.

GEORGE   It's on Tuesday nights.

DAVID   Yeh, beginning of the week, generally, I tend to ... you know ... (*Points at the CD player.*) Ravel.

GEORGE   Sorry?

DAVID   I love Ravel.

GEORGE   Really. Yes, my wife's very keen ... at the moment ...

DAVID   I lent her a CD. A while back. (GEORGE *looks up.*) This one, I think. Are you using it for your farce? (GEORGE *stares.*) It's perfect for farce. Perpetuum mobile! Perpetual movement.

GEORGE   Yes, I know what it means.

(GEORGE *presses a button on his remote. The music jumps forward to Offenbach, 'Gaîté Parisienne'.* DAVID *listens to it, frowning.*)

DAVID What's this?

GEORGE Offenbach. How d'you know what I'm writing?

DAVID (*brazen*) I read it. Yesterday. D'you mind? Anne said it was OK.

GEORGE Did she.

DAVID (*re: pages on* GEORGE'S *table*) You've written some more?

GEORGE It's a first draft. I don't like people reading drafts.

DAVID I didn't read it exactly. I skimmed it.

GEORGE Has Anne read it?

DAVID Um . . . She said she was going to . . .

(GEORGE *stares, then rises decisively and exits to the house, pulling up his trousers as they fall.*)

DAVID (*mischievous*) I'm sure she loved it.

GEORGE (*off*) Anne! (*Fainter.*) Anne!

ANNE (*off*) What?

(*While* GEORGE *and* ANNE (MARIANNE *in acts one and two*) *have an inaudible conversation off-stage,* DAVID *peruses the pages on* GEORGE'S *table.*)

ANNE (*enters at speed carrying various items of clothing*) That character is me! Again! Another miserable, nagging battleaxe!

(GEORGE *enters, pursuing her.*)

GEORGE	I've borrowed some minor details! That's all!
ANNE	Bollocks!
	(*She exits to the hall.*)
GEORGE	Why do you think that every wife character I write is you?!
	(GEORGE *exits in pursuit.* DAVID *switches off the music in order to eavesdrop.*)
ANNE	(*off*) Why is every wife character you write a battleaxe?!
GEORGE	(*off*) It's a comedy staple!
ANNE	(*off*) It's not just me! We're all in there! Even your idiot therapist!
GEORGE	(*off*) What therapist?
ANNE	(*off*) All right, your ex-therapist! (*Enters, without the clothes, still walking at speed.*) Ben-*WAA*, for God's sake! (*She turns suddenly and confronts him as he enters.*) Can't you make something up?! You're a writer! You're supposed to make things up!
GEORGE	It's mostly made up!
ANNE	You even used me *complaining* about the fact that you don't make things up!
GEORGE	What?!
ANNE	'You should pay me royalties'. I said that to you! When we had that argument. In that awful restaurant. I said 'you should pay me royalties' and you said 'that's what I've been doing ever since we were married'!

GEORGE I was quoting Feydeau! He said that to his wife! It was in your book!

ANNE What book?!

GEORGE Did you not give me a book?! For my birthday?! On Feydeau?!

ANNE No.

DAVID That was me. I gave it to you.

GEORGE (*beat*) Well, whatever ...

DAVID It was my idea. In fact. A farce about Feydeau.

(*Beat.*)

GEORGE We had a conversation. I don't remember it being your idea.

DAVID (*quickly, almost rehearsed*) You told me you were enjoying the book and I said 'his life was so farcical, you could almost write a farce about it' and you said that was a good idea but you didn't have time so you said 'why don't you write it yourself?'.

(*Beat. They stare at him.*)

GEORGE Why on earth would you want to write a farce?

DAVID (*shrug, defensive*) Because I think I could make it interesting. And relevant.

GEORGE Farce is supposed to be funny.

DAVID Yes. And that.

ANNE Are you two going to fight over such a stupid idea?

DAVID	I don't think it's stupid.
GEORGE	Can you give us a moment? Please?
	(*Pause.*)
DAVID	Sure.
	(*Provocatively, he gathers up* GEORGE'S *papers and exits to the house.*)
GEORGE	(*following*) Hey! I'm working on that! (*He returns to the room, still holding up his trousers.*) What is he doing here?!
ANNE	How should I know?
GEORGE	You told him he could read my script!
ANNE	If it was his idea . . .
GEORGE	It's only a couple of scenes! I'm not even sure if I'll finish . . . In fact! Maybe I'll throw it away! Is that what you want? Shall I tear it to pieces?! (*He moves to pursue* DAVID.)
ANNE	Are you having an affair?
	(*He turns and, forgetting to hold up his trousers, they fall down.*)
ANNE	(*incensed*) Did you do that deliberately?!
GEORGE	(*pulling them up*) Sorry. They're farce trousers.
ANNE	You're taking the piss!
GEORGE	They have weights around the top. So they fall down easily. You think I'm having an affair?!

ANNE	(*takes a breath*) When I got home. From Aunt Irene's. (*With his remote control,* GEORGE *turns the Offenbach back on.*) There was someone in the house. And you'd been out. (*She becomes aware of the music.*) What are you doing?!
GEORGE	I don't want David hearing our business.
ANNE	(*grimacing*) What on earth . . . ?!
GEORGE	It's Offenbach. For my play.
ANNE	Turn it off! (*He does so.*) I'm trying to have a serious conversation!
GEORGE	Sorry.
ANNE	There was someone in the house! Wasn't there? And you'd been out with Ben the night before. For Christ's sake, it's all in your stupid play!
GEORGE	La Dame de chez Maxim.
ANNE	(*over*) It was that bimbo actress, wasn't it? Christine. Cécile. Whatever her name is. I even found her scarf!
GEORGE	That was mine.
ANNE	Bollocks!
GEORGE	(*loudly*) La Dame de chez Maxim!
ANNE	What?
GEORGE	It's a play! By Feydeau! And that's what happens. Beginning of act one. The husband's asleep on the sofa, his wife comes home and there's this woman in his bed.

(*Pause.*)

ANNE	You mean, you just stole that scene?
GEORGE	It's an hommage.
ANNE	Omage? What is that, French for stealing?
GEORGE	It means showing respect by ...
ANNE	Homage! (*Pronounced hommidge.*) The word is homage, you pompous twit!
GEORGE	Homage, hommage ...
ANNE	So, what are you saying? There's nothing going on? With you and that actress?
GEORGE	Nothing. What's going on with you and David?
ANNE	What?
GEORGE	Has he completed your education in French classical music?
ANNE	What are you talking about?
GEORGE	He's lending you Ravel CDs.
ANNE	Oh, I see! Does that explain the Oftenbark?
GEORGE	What?
ANNE	You don't want to use Ravel any more.
GEORGE	I can't. It's too modern. It's nineteen-twenty-something.
ANNE	(*scrutinising him*) No, you're jealous. Aren't you?
GEORGE	Jealous?
ANNE	That explains why you hate him so much.

GEORGE	Hate him?!
ANNE	You've turned him into an utter idiot.
GEORGE	You mean Louis Levasseur?
ANNE	Those are his stupid trousers, I suppose.
GEORGE	Personally, I think it's a rather favourable portrait.
ANNE	Totally one-dimensional!
GEORGE	Farce characters are one-dimensional! There's no psychological complexity.
ANNE	What if I sleep with him?! Tonight! What about that?!
GEORGE	There's no need.
ANNE	What?
GEORGE	I'm not screwing anyone.
ANNE	No *'need'*? There's no *'need'* for me to sleep with someone else? Don't you even entertain the possibility that I might actually *like* to sleep with someone else?!
GEORGE	Not David, for Christ's sake.
ANNE	(*over*) That I might, in fact, on occasion, *YEARN* to sleep with someone else?! Someone who doesn't do the same things to me, in the same order! Often while wearing socks with Disney characters on them!
GEORGE	(*hurt*) Well, I apologise for my poor performance.
ANNE	We all have the same temptations! And nobody's one-dimensional! Not even you!

(*Doorbell.*)

GEORGE Yvette!

(*Pause.* ANNE *takes a deep breath, holding back tears.*)

ANNE I feel desperate...

GEORGE I'll throw the socks away.

ANNE I don't care about the socks!

GEORGE Well, you clearly do.

(*She takes another deep breath.*)

ANNE (*matter-of-fact*) I shout. And I shout. Because I'm not being heard. And I'm beginning to hate myself. (*Pause.*) We need to talk. And we can't talk if we can't at least, first of all, be honest with each other. If this marriage means anything to you... Tell me the truth. Please.

GEORGE About what?

ANNE That actress. For a start.

GEORGE I don't even know her! I've only met her once!

(*Pause.* ANNE *stares at him, then heaves a sigh of resignation. She raises her hands to her face. He approaches her slowly and wraps his arms around her.* BEN (DIDIER *in acts one and two*) *appears unnoticed in the doorway to the hall. He is dressed smartly in casual clothes but looks ill and is shaking almost imperceptibly.* GEORGE *and* ANNE *stand motionless for a moment until she raises a knee sharply between his legs. As he groans and falls slowly onto the floor*, ANNE *exits quickly to the hall, barely registering Ben's presence.*)

BEN My God, she attacked you?!

(BEN *closes the door and tries to help* GEORGE *to his feet but* GEORGE *holds up a hand to keep him away.*)

GEORGE No, just a minor . . . knee in the groin . . .

BEN I feel so guilty! (GEORGE *looks up at him quizzically.*) She rang me earlier. Asked if you were screwing Christine.

GEORGE What did you tell her?

BEN How should I know? (*Beat.*) But I said you've had quite a few meetings recently.

(GEORGE *groans and lowers his head into his hands.*)

BEN Are you screwing her?

GEORGE No. I'm not.

BEN Your wife thinks you are.

GEORGE My bloody play! I don't believe it!

BEN Has Christine called you?

GEORGE Why would she call me?

BEN I saw her this morning. Drove around to her house.

GEORGE You what?

BEN I was in a state. After talking to Anne. I needed to know what's going on.

GEORGE Was her husband there?

BEN	Apparently. But I don't think he saw me.
GEORGE	I thought they were going on holiday. To sort out their problems.
BEN	They couldn't agree where to go.
GEORGE	Listen! Leave me out of this! All right? I don't want anything to do with it!
BEN	If she does drop around here, go easy on her because she's really (*Shaky hand gesture.*) . . .

(GEORGE, *still suffering, perches carefully on a chair.*)

GEORGE	Why would she come here?
BEN	Um . . . She said she might.
GEORGE	And I hope you told her not to! (BEN *stares blankly.*) Ben, my marriage is on the brink here!
BEN	She won't! I'm sure she won't.
GEORGE	Ring her! And tell her! She can't come here!
BEN	Yes. All right. (*Suddenly wants to leave.*) I should go. I've got an emergency consultation this evening. (*He checks his watch.*) Christ! Fifteen minutes!

(BEN, *light-headed, sits for a moment.*)

GEORGE	Ben, you're in no state to psychoanalyse anyone. As usual.
BEN	(*taken aback*) I'm fine. What d'you mean?
GEORGE	You're shaking.

BEN	No, that's just a minor side effect.
GEORGE	Of what?
BEN	I'm coming off Prozac at the moment.
	(DAVID *enters from the house, flicking through the script.*)
DAVID	This is not bad. It just needs a bit of focus.
GEORGE	I suppose you hate the Levasseur character.
DAVID	Why?
GEORGE	A bit... exaggerated.
DAVID	Not really. I know people like that. If you want to collaborate...
GEORGE	(*thrown momentarily, he stifles a laugh*) No. I don't.
DAVID	This was my idea.
GEORGE	I don't remember that.
DAVID	And I can improve it. D'you know much about the Belle Epoque?
GEORGE	I know enough.
DAVID	(*reads*) 'He strangles Chambraud with his belt.' Did they have belts? I thought it was all braces?
GEORGE	It's a first draft. I'm not even sure if I'll continue.
DAVID	Hotel at the End of Civilisation.
GEORGE	(*stares*) What is that?
DAVID	It's a title.

GEORGE	Jesus . . .
DAVID	Hotel Terminus. Terminal. End of. Paris at the end of the Belle Epoque. The Banquet Years, bourgeois debauchery, a society in moral meltdown. Then the first world war comes along . . .
GEORGE	I want 'monkey' in the title.
BEN	Monkey Business.
DAVID	That's the Marx Brothers.
GEORGE	Monkey Nuts.
DAVID	(*grimace*) No, no.
GEORGE	Nuts means crazy. Also testicles. Animal urges. That's what all farce is about. People pretending to be civilised but actually controlled by their . . .
BEN	Their subconscious.
GEORGE	Their monkey nuts.
	(*Doorbell.*)
GEORGE	If that's Christine . . .
BEN	No, I'm sure it's not.
GEORGE	. . . just get rid of her.
	(BEN *exits to the hall.*)
GEORGE	This jacket . . . ! My life turns into farce when I wear it!
	(GEORGE *removes his jacket and hangs it over a different chair.*)

DAVID	It's not the jacket. It's your lifestyle.
GEORGE	(*searching the room for something*) What d'you mean?
DAVID	Big house. Big family.
GEORGE	Yes, all right . . .
DAVID	French au pair.
GEORGE	Yvette!

(GEORGE *exits to the house.* DAVID *follows him.*)

DAVID	(*as he goes*) It's a modern day farce.

(CHRISTINE (CÉCILE *in acts one and two*) *enters, followed by* BEN *who is trying to restrain her. She is wearing sexy clothes including mid-length skirt and boots. She is also wearing the same scarf as in act one. She seems slightly odd, unfocussed.*)

BEN	Christine! You can't go in there! I'm taking you home!
CHRISTINE	(*determined*) I want to speak to him. Where is he?
BEN	(*anxious*) His wife is here!
CHRISTINE	Good. I want to meet her.

(CHRISTINE *peeks into the bathroom.*)

BEN	That's just the bathroom.
CHRISTINE	Where is he? Where's Georgie-Porgie?
BEN	(*takes hold of her arms*) You need to leave! Right now! (*Staring into her eyes.*) Are you drunk?

CHRISTINE	No. Just a bit high.
BEN	(*sarcastic*) Wonderful.
GEORGE	(*off*) David, I haven't got time . . .
DAVID	(*off*) Monkey de Sade. That's a great title.
	(BEN *bundles* CHRISTINE *into the bathroom and closes the door.* GEORGE *enters, still looking for something, now frowning, frustrated.* DAVID *follows.*)
GEORGE	It's not a farce title.
DAVID	Why not?
GEORGE	Monkey Nuts is a farce title. Monkey Business, Monkey's Uncle . . .
DAVID	All right, Monkey's Uncle. Boring. But better than Monkey Nuts.
GEORGE	(*searching the room*) There's already a farce called Monkey's Uncle. Nineteen-seventies. American. (*Calls off-stage:*) Yvette!
DAVID	(*becoming annoyed*) Well, that doesn't count. How can you worry about stealing a title! You stole the whole idea from me!
GEORGE	No, I didn't. Yvette! Where are my damned trousers?!
DAVID	Half of what you've written is stolen from Feydeau!
GEORGE	It's *about* Feydeau!
DAVID	(*over*) And that monkey audition thing! I'm sure I've seen that in Sergeant Bilko! Most of your sitcom plots are stolen from Bilko! Or Hancock! Or . . .

ACT THREE

GEORGE
(*still searching*) I thought you didn't watch my sitcoms!

DAVID
You can't call it Monkey Nuts! That's so simplistic!

GEORGE
Yvette!!

DAVID
'We're just monkeys – dominated by sexual urges – society is irrelevant.' That's such a right-wing thesis.

GEORGE
That's what farce is about! It's about human nature!

(GEORGE *exits at speed to the house.*)

DAVID
No! It's about human nurture!

(DAVID *follows* GEORGE *into the house. A moment later,* BEN *peeks into the room. The coast is clear.*)

BEN
(*urgent whisper*) All right, come on.

(*He leads* CHRISTINE *by the hand towards the hall. She notices* ANNE'S *cardigan and pulls her hand free.*)

CHRISTINE
Oh, look ... (*She tries it on.*)

BEN
Christine ... !

CHRISTINE
God, it's gorgeous. Feels like ...

BEN
Cashmere.

CHRISTINE
Money. Feels like money. (*She sees the velvet smoking jacket.*) Wow, look at this! Try it on.

BEN
No!

CHRISTINE
Just for a second.

BEN	(*becoming slightly hysterical*) Christine, I have a client waiting for me with borderline psychosis!
CHRISTINE	I'll go if you try this on.
	(*She helps him to put on the jacket. She is very tactile with him which calms him slightly.*)
CHRISTINE	How about that?!
BEN	Let's go! Please!
	(*Pause.* CHRISTINE *shrugs and exits to the hall. She is still wearing* ANNE'S *cardigan.*)
BEN	Christine! The cardigan!
	(*He chases her out.* GEORGE *returns from the house with a pair of non-descript modern trousers.* DAVID *follows.*)
GEORGE	All right, I've got work to do. (*He begins putting on the trousers.*)
DAVID	Feydeau was writing about a particular society! An age of bourgeois decadence!
GEORGE	No, actually, it was an age of peace and prosperity.
DAVID	(*over*) He left his family and lived in a shag pad in the Hotel Terminus for ten years! Finally caught syphilis from one of those posh Parisian prostitutes. 'Les grandes horizontales.'
GEORGE	(*loudly, struggling to put on his trousers*) Nobody's interested in Belle Epoque Paris! I'm not writing a history play! I'm writing about farce! Farce is universal!

DAVID	(*racing*) Feydeau is not universal! Nobody produced a Feydeau play in . . . in Maoist China!
GEORGE	Nobody produced anything in Maoist China!
DAVID	(*over*) But he's relevant to us! To now! That's the point! Just look around you! This is Belle Epoque Paris!
GEORGE	Where?!
DAVID	(*over*) Consumerism gone mad! Everyone's on the make! Everyone's shopping! Buying big houses and filling them full of junk! No one has time to think about anything! No one even pauses for breath! Perpetuum mobile!
GEORGE	Will you calm down?
DAVID	So, we're just farce characters! Reacting to events! With no self-awareness! No better than animals!
GEORGE	All right, enough . . .
DAVID	Farce is the modern world! Unless you stop and get off!
GEORGE	Yes, I'd like to.
DAVID	Assert your humanity! Like The Rhinosceros. Ionesco.
GEORGE	What?
	(GEORGE *exits to the house.* DAVID *follows.*)
DAVID	(*as he goes*) Ionesco was very influenced by Feydeau.
GEORGE	(*off, sarcastic*) Fascinating.

(BEN *peers in. He enters cautiously and hangs* ANNE'S *cardigan over the back of a chair near the table – but he doesn't take off the smoking jacket.*)

BEN We better go.

CHRISTINE You said her car's gone.

BEN Well, what if she comes back? Christine, you can't just turn up at someone's house! If you want to speak to him, then call him.

(CHRISTINE *notices the script on the table and peruses it.*)

BEN That's his new play. Maybe a part for you.

CHRISTINE Apparently not. (*Beat.*) Don't care. He's a crap writer anyway.

BEN What happened with you two? Did you sleep with him?

CHRISTINE Once. (*They stare.*) Jealous? (*Beat.*) You love it, don't you? Hearing my stories.

BEN Not particularly.

CHRISTINE But they make you horny.

BEN The hotel?

CHRISTINE No. The night before. He brought me here. His wife was at her Aunt's.

BEN Christ! Did you do it in the marital bed?

CHRISTINE (*holding eye contact*) No. The sofa. The stairs. The kitchen floor. (*Beat.*) In here too. He had me bent over this table.

(Beat. She slowly turns away from him and bends seductively over the table. He watches, suffering. She places her handbag on the table and, waving her backside in his direction, removes some items including a couple of bank notes and a small container filled with cocaine. She tips some out onto the table and begins arranging it into lines with a bank note.)

BEN   You can't do that here!

CHRISTINE   Want some?

BEN   Oh, sure! I'll take some for my psychotic client too!

CHRISTINE   Probably do him good.

(She takes some of the powder between thumb and forefinger and inhales it sharply up one nostril. She closes her eyes and takes a deep breath. She arches her back and her hips sway rhythmically.)

CHRISTINE   Why don't you stick it in me?

BEN   *(annoyed)* For Christ's sake . . .

(She begins slowly to remove her knickers from under her skirt.)

BEN   If we were somewhere safe! Where no one could possibly walk in on us! You wouldn't be interested at all! Would you?! *(She stuffs her white knickers into* ANNE'S *cardigan pocket.)* Don't do that! That's just childish!

(He moves to retrieve the knickers but she grabs his hand and places it on her backside. She resumes her position, bent over the table.)

CHRISTINE   Come on, tiger, I know you want to.

BEN	(*desperate*) You know what your problem is? You think sex is bad! You think your desires are bad! You want to be discovered. And punished. Don't you? But you're wrong! Everyone has desires! We all do! (*He looks around at the doors anxiously.*) We just keep them hidden! Behind a socially acceptable persona!
CHRISTINE	Shut up and stick it in me.

(*She begins rolling a twenty-pound note into a narrow tube.* BEN *glances around at the doors and, with trembling fingers, he begins to undo his trousers.*)

BEN	I can see him in my waiting room! Getting more and more psychotic!
DAVID	(*off*) This is the ending! All right?
GEORGE	(*off*) Will you leave me alone?

(BEN *grabs* CHRISTINE *from behind and manhandles her into the bathroom closing the door behind him.*)

CHRISTINE	(*as she goes*) Can't help yourself, can you?

(GEORGE *enters, followed by* DAVID, *who shuts the door deliberately.* GEORGE *sits and begins sorting his papers.*)

DAVID	(*possessed*) Just listen for a second! Feydeau caught syphilis. Ended up demented in the nuthouse. One morning they found him grazing on the grass, believing he's a cow! That's the ending, right there!
GEORGE	How is that an ending?
DAVID	A life of bourgeois depravity! He ends up a cow eating grass! Echoes of Ionesco!

GEORGE	What happened to your global warming play?

DAVID	Too depressing. I need to write something people actually want to see. For a change.

GEORGE	Selling out, are you?

DAVID	Commercial but not mindless! Subvert the genre! Like Joe Orton. Dario Fo.

GEORGE	You have to be able to write the genre before you can subvert it.

DAVID	You don't think I can?!

GEORGE	D'you think comedy is easy?! D'you think farce is easy?!

DAVID	I can write comedy!

GEORGE	Well, then, write it! And forget about 'subverting' it!

DAVID	What's the point of doing a farce, an outmoded genre, if it's not saying anything?!

GEORGE	Farce is not intellectual! You said so yourself! Farce characters don't think! They just react!

DAVID	(*losing his temper*) But it's a farce about Feydeau! The authorial voice is actually a sodding character! So it's easy! You have Feydeau telling his wife about farce – 'it's not real, I don't really sleep with whores, blah blah blah' – in order to distract her from the half-naked whore sneaking out of the room behind her! Listen, I'm not giving you all my ideas . . .

GEORGE	Oh, you think I'd actually use all that?! You think I'd use your 'Feydeau pretending to be a cow' idea?!
DAVID	How else would you end it?
GEORGE	It's a farce! You can't suddenly switch to the garden of a mental asylum!
DAVID	Of course you can! This is not sitcom! This is theatre! You can do what you like! A few sound effects! Change the lighting! Last act, darkness. Birds chirping, dawn chorus. Lights slowly rise . . .
	(BEN *enters unobtrusively, closing the bathroom door behind him. He watches, waiting sheepishly for a moment to interrupt. He is still wearing the smoking jacket.*)
GEORGE	Farce is all about the set! It's all about doors! You know, there are two hundred and seventy-nine entrances and exits in L'Hôtel du Libre-Echange.
DAVID	You don't need doors! Just sound effects!
GEORGE	Of course you need doors! You don't even know the basics!
DAVID	No, look! Listen! Go over there! (*He indicates the door to the house.*)
GEORGE	Why?
BEN	(*soft*) George?
DAVID	Go over there! Just for a second!
GEORGE	No!
DAVID	(*sigh*) Please! Go over there for a second. (GEORGE *shuffles reluctantly over to the door.*) I

ACT THREE

saw this at the Orange Tree. I'm the stage manager. In the wings.

BEN George, I need a word ...

DAVID Ben! Just a minute! Now, pretend to open the door! (GEORGE *opens the door.*) No! *Pretend* to open it!

GEORGE Will you calm down!

DAVID *Pretend* to open it. *Mime* opening it.

GEORGE You want me to *mime*?!

DAVID Yes! Mime! (GEORGE *extravagantly mimes opening the door as* DAVID *tries to open the drawer in the table.*) I don't believe it! Why would you lock a stupid little drawer?! (*He tries to yank it open.*)

GEORGE Don't! You'll break the bloody thing! (*He takes the tiny key from the inside pocket of the jacket* BEN *is wearing.*)

BEN (*more assertive*) George, we have a problem here ...

GEORGE (*unlocking the drawer*) Hold on a minute.

DAVID All right, try it again.

GEORGE It's theatre. Not radio. You can't use sound effects.

DAVID Just go over there. (GEORGE *sighs, returns to the door and mimes opening it.* DAVID *noisily opens the drawer.*) Now shut it. (*The door opens.* YVETTE *enters, closing the door behind her.*) For Christ's sake ... Sorry! Can you give us a moment, please?

YVETTE (*affronted*) Excusez moi!

(YVETTE *exits to the hall, closing the door behind her.*)

DAVID: All right. (GEORGE *mimes opening the door as* DAVID *shuts the drawer.*) What are you doing?!

GEORGE: What?

DAVID: The door was open! You just opened it again!

BEN: George!

GEORGE: (*indicating the door*) It's closed!

DAVID: (*losing it*) The *imaginary* door was open! My drawer was open! (*He opens the drawer again.*) All right! Open! OK? Now shut it!

(YVETTE *enters from the hall.*)

YVETTE: Madame est revenue.

(*In quick succession,* BEN *exits to the bathroom, closing the door behind him,* YVETTE *exits to the house and* ANNE *enters from the hall carrying some shopping in a plastic bag. She closes the door behind her. Looks are exchanged.*)

ANNE: Am I interrupting . . . ?

(*After a pause,* DAVID *slams the drawer in and out a few times until it breaks and won't go back in. He exits to the hall, slamming the door behind him.* ANNE *puts the shopping down near the table.*)

ANNE: What's his problem?

GEORGE: (*sigh*) He wants to collaborate. Maybe I'll just give it to him. I'm fed up with it.

ANNE: (*guilty*) Are you all right? Did I hurt you?

GEORGE	No, I'm fine.
ANNE	I broke my promise.
GEORGE	What promise?
ANNE	That I'd never hit you again.
GEORGE	(*shrug*) You didn't hit me.
ANNE	(*beat*) Anyway, I'm going to Mum's. So I got you a few things.

(*She tries to close the drawer but it is stuck.*)

ANNE I think he's broken this.

(*She examines it from the inside and discovers a note.*)

GEORGE (*realising what it is*) Um . . .

ANNE (*reads*) "My dearest, try as I might, I can't resist you. For some strange reason, my heart beats more quickly when you're near. I will see you tonight at the hotel, as you suggest."

GEORGE That's for my play. (*She stares.*) I like to act things out.

ANNE This is not your handwriting.

GEORGE (*takes and studies it*) No, I was . . . writing in character.

(*Noises from the bathroom.*)

ANNE Who's in there?

GEORGE Ben, I think.

(ANNE takes a deep breath and tries to stay calm.)

ANNE I have to just go. I have to get out of here.

GEORGE Anne, please . . . I wish I'd never started that bloody play! I really do! But I never thought, for one second, that you'd imagine I was stupid enough to write about my own infidelities! Who the hell would do that?

ANNE Was she here? That time. Did you bring her here?

GEORGE Who? *(ANNE stares.)* No. She's never been here. I promise! On my mother's grave!

ANNE Your mother's still alive.

GEORGE She bought a cemetery plot last week.

ANNE Listen, I need to go. So . . . *(She lifts her shopping onto a chair.)* I got a few things. For you. And Yvette. Toothpaste. Bread. But you'll need to do a shop. Maybe tomorrow. And the bin men are coming. Don't forget to put out the bottles. It's no use asking Yvette.

GEORGE *(dawning realisation)* What are you talking about? Where are you going?

(More noises from the bathroom – a number of objects knocked onto the floor.)

ANNE For God's sake . . . *(She knocks.)* Ben? Are you all right?

BEN *(off)* Yes, fine! I slipped.

GEORGE *(oblivious to BEN)* Anne. *(He turns her towards him.)* Where are you going?

ANNE I told you. My mother's.

GEORGE	For how long?
ANNE	A few days. Maybe more.
GEORGE	Where are the kids?
ANNE	I took them this afternoon. (*Beat.*) I had a feeling you wouldn't notice.
GEORGE	Well, I thought it was quiet...
ANNE	I think we should split up. (*Beat.*) And I have to be here. With the kids. So... (*Pause.* GEORGE *stares.* ANNE *almost cries but stops herself.*) If I stay with Mum for a while, it'll give you some time...
GEORGE	(*beat*) To do what?
ANNE	To move out.
	(GEORGE *stares, shell-shocked. Pause.*)
GEORGE	I don't understand.
	(ANNE *is losing the battle with her emotions. She exits quickly to the house.* GEORGE *sits, staring.* BEN *emerges cautiously but with some urgency. His hair is a mess and his trousers are undone. He is still wearing the smoking jacket. He glances back into the bathroom, then quietly closes the door.*)
BEN	She's not well.
GEORGE	Who?
BEN	Christine. She's done a lot of coke. (GEORGE *stares.*) And God knows what else.
GEORGE	She's in there?!

BEN	(*trying to refasten his flies*) She attacked me. Then she passed out.
GEORGE	Did you hit her?!
BEN	No! She passed out! (*He is struggling with his flies.*) These are ruined ...
GEORGE	For God's sake!
	(GEORGE *attends to* BEN'S *flies as* ANNE *enters from the house with a toilet bag.*)
ANNE	(*thrown*) What are you doing?
BEN	Oh! Hi!
GEORGE	We're just ... (*Stares at* BEN.) Trying out a few things. For the play. (*He makes* BEN'S *hair even more messy.*) Perfect. (*An idea occurs.*) In fact ...! (*He fetches the farce trousers.*) Why don't you try these on?
BEN	(*beat*) OK. (*He removes his own trousers.*)
ANNE	Unbelievable. It's all you care about, isn't it? Your work.
	(ANNE *marches towards the bathroom.* GEORGE *darts in front of her.*)
GEORGE	Sorry, I'm bursting.
ANNE	I just need a few things.
GEORGE	I won't be long.
	(*He exits to the bathroom. Uncomfortable pause as* BEN *struggles to put on the farce trousers.*)
BEN	So, how are you?
ANNE	(*beat*) I've been better.

(She puts on her cardigan. Sharp intake of breath from BEN. ANNE *notices the state of the table.)*

ANNE Look at this mess. I don't know why I bother ... *(As she begins tidying the table,* BEN *tries to manoeuvre himself into a position from which he can extract* CHRISTINE'S *knickers from* ANNE'S *cardigan pocket.)* It's not easy, Ben. When your marriage goes wrong. And stays wrong.

BEN *(not listening)* Yes.

ANNE You end up feeling so down about yourself, it's almost impossible to imagine you'd be okay on your own. (BEN *slowly pulls the knickers from her pocket.)* But I was once. I have to remember that. *(She notices the cocaine.)* What is this? Salt?

(She picks some up and throws it over her left shoulder into BEN'S *face. He yelps and retreats, but manages to stuff the knickers into his own jacket pocket.)*

ANNE Oh, God! Sorry! I didn't see you there. Are you all right? *(She knocks on the bathroom door.)* George? (BEN *exits unnoticed to the hall. She knocks again.)* George!

GEORGE *(off)* Hold on.

ANNE *(sees that* BEN *has vanished)* Ben?

(She exits to the house. GEORGE *enters warily, closing the bathroom door behind him. He tiptoes to the door to the house.)*

GEORGE Ben?

(BEN *enters from the hall, hand over one eye.)*

GEORGE Christine's out cold.

BEN	I'll carry her. To my car.
GEORGE	Not yet! Anne's just leaving.
BEN	She's unconscious! She's not going to say anything! Tell Anne she followed me here and passed out.
GEORGE	I just promised, on my mother's grave!, that she'd never been here!
BEN	Your mother died?!
GEORGE	Give me two minutes!
	(GEORGE *pushes him into the bathroom and closes the door.* ANNE *returns.*)
ANNE	(*disturbed*) Where's Ben?
GEORGE	(*indicates the bathroom*) In there. He's fine.
ANNE	Christ, I keep hurting people.
GEORGE	Shall we . . . Should we . . . sit down . . . ? (*He indicates the door to the house.*)
ANNE	What for?
GEORGE	Well, he might be a while . . .
ANNE	I have to go.
GEORGE	Can you go upstairs?
ANNE	I mean, I have to leave.
GEORGE	Oh.
ANNE	I really do. (*Deep breath, holding back tears.*) Because I feel like I'm losing it, George. (*More noises from the bathroom which distract* GEORGE.) And I'm so suspicious! All the

	time! Even when I read your writing. It's crazy!
GEORGE	Can we go and sit down?
	(*He takes her hand to lead her out of the room but she just pulls him to her and hugs him tightly. He tries to move her towards the house but she is a dead weight.*)
GEORGE	You're not going to kick me again?
ANNE	No. I promise.
	(*Noises off.* GEORGE *reaches for the remote control and turns the music on to cover the noise. Offenbach, 'Gaîté Parisienne' is heard again.*)
GEORGE	Shall we dance?
ANNE	No, thanks.
	(BEN *pokes his head into the room.* GEORGE *waves him back into the bathroom.*)
ANNE	I don't know why it bothered me so much. Your play. It just seemed so real. Somehow.
GEORGE	Listen, I may have used things . . . Domestic details. But . . .
	(BEN *enters silently, carrying an unconscious* CHRISTINE *in his arms.* GEORGE *panics for a moment but hugs* ANNE *to himself and slowly turns the music up until it is rather loud. He tries to keep talking, a certain desperation in his voice.*)
GEORGE	But . . . it's not real. Farce is not real. That's the point. It's . . . um . . .

(BEN *heads for the door to the hall and his trousers begin to fall down. He cannot pull them up. They fall down to his ankles and he continues slowly with very short steps.*)

GEORGE It's not the surface. If you know what I mean. It's below. It's inner desires acted out. Like melodrama.

ANNE Well, at least melodrama is serious. Farce is a joke. It felt like you were making a joke of our marriage.

(BEN *is making very slow silent progress.*)

GEORGE No, but I think melodrama misses something! Because basically . . . We're just animals who dress up in fancy clothing and pretend we're not animals! And that's funny! Don't you think? That conflict! Between civilisation and human nature!

(*As* BEN *walks past,* GEORGE *turns slightly so* ANNE *remains facing in the right direction.*)

ANNE Maybe there's a conflict between marriage and human nature.

GEORGE (*shrug*) Well, I wouldn't say that . . .

(*Doorbell.* BEN *turns back towards the bathroom. Behind* ANNE'S *back,* GEORGE *indicates to* BEN *the door to the house.*)

ANNE You think men are naturally promiscuous. Don't you?

(BEN *walks as fast as possible (ie, not very) towards the house. The music is now rather loud.* GEORGE *turns* ANNE *in a different direction.* ANNE *is becoming unnerved by George's embrace and is now ready to be released.*)

GEORGE	Well, maybe we all are. Maybe we all have the same temptations. Like you said. And we're all ... complicated. We all have ... perhaps ... conflicting motivations ... But I'm writing a farce! So it's simple! I have to get into that mentality! (*He turns the music up even louder.*) You know? Like if you watch one, you're sitting there with your wife, in perfect safety! Vicariously enjoying the pleasures and the dangers of adultery!

(BEN *carries* CHRISTINE *out to the house.*)

ANNE	Can you let me go now?
GEORGE	I love this music! Don't you?
ANNE	Not really, no.

(*He pulls her into a dance.*)

ANNE	George, please.

(BEN *returns quickly, struggling with his trousers.* GEORGE *spins* ANNE *in a different direction.* BEN *darts back into the bathroom.*)

ANNE	George!
GEORGE	Sorry.

(*He releases her.*)

ANNE	That's enough. Can you switch it off?

(*He does so.* ANNE *knocks on the bathroom door.*)

BEN	(*off, high-pitched*) Just a moment.

(*Pause.* ANNE *tries not to look at* GEORGE.)

ANNE	I'll call you. In a ... In a while.

(BEN *emerges from the bathroom carrying his jeans (in which he has hidden* CHRISTINE'S *handbag) and the smoking jacket. Doorbell.*)

ANNE — Yvette!

BEN — (*breathless*) Well, I better be off . . .

GEORGE — Oh, okay.

ANNE — Are you all right?

BEN — Yes, fine. See you later.

(YVETTE *enters from the house and shuffles across the stage.*)

GEORGE — My jacket?

BEN — Oh. Right.

(*He extricates* GEORGE'S *jacket from the other items and hands it to him.* CHRISTINE'S *scarf falls onto the floor.* GEORGE *puts the jacket on.* YVETTE *exits to the hall.*)

ANNE — What's that?

BEN — What? That. Oh, that's . . . my scarf. (*He tries to pick it up and put it on.*)

GEORGE — No, I think it's mine.

ANNE — It's Christine's. Isn't it?

BEN — I don't think so.

ANNE — (*peers into the empty bathroom*) Is she here?

GEORGE — What d'you mean 'is she here'?

ANNE — What d'you think I mean?!

GEORGE	You mean hidden? Like some sort of . . . farce cliché?
ANNE	(*to* BEN) Where is she?!
	(YVETTE *wanders in from the hall.*)
GEORGE	Didn't you tell me she was on holiday?
BEN	Oh! Yes. She went to . . . France. This morning. With her husband.
YVETTE	Il y a un homme ici qui cherche sa femme.
	(*Pause. Stunned silence.* YVETTE *exits to the house.*)
GEORGE	What did she say?
	(ALAN (HABILLOT *in acts one and two*) *enters.* BEN *ducks under the table.*)
ALAN	Hello, George! So sorry to burst in like this!
GEORGE	(*shakes his hand*) Alan! Nice to see you again.
ALAN	I won't stay. I'm just looking for my wife.
GEORGE	Oh, really? No, she's not here.
	(GEORGE *hangs his smoking jacket over a chair next to the table to help obscure* BEN.)
ALAN	Oh, right. Well, sorry to bother you. Um . . . There's a car out there. Which . . . seems familiar.
GEORGE	Oh! Yes. It belongs to a friend of mine. But he's not here at the moment. We're . . . looking after his car . . . Shall we sit down? (*He indicates the door to the house.*)

ANNE	(*offers a chair near the table*) Yes, here we go! Would you like a tea or a coffee?
ALAN	(*sits*) No, thanks. I'm not stopping. By the way, I'm enjoying your sitcom.
GEORGE	Oh. Thanks.
ALAN	(*re: the script on the table*) Is that a new episode?
GEORGE	No. It's a play. A farce.
ALAN	Oh! I remember you saying...
ANNE	In fact, this is his farce jacket!

(ANNE *removes the jacket from the chair and puts it on* GEORGE.)

ALAN	Oh! Excellent.
ANNE	It helps him get into the right mentality. You know? Somewhere between idiot and ...imbecile.
GEORGE	(*laughs, points at his wife*) Very funny.
ALAN	Have you got an ending yet?
GEORGE	Not yet. Maybe the...er... Maybe Feydeau...in the sanatorium. Demented. Believing he's a cow.
ANNE	What did I tell you?
GEORGE	Actually, I'm a bit busy...
ALAN	Yes, sure!
ANNE	(*raises a hand to keep* ALAN *in his chair*) No, no! Stay for a bit. Go on, George! Tell us. Tell us more.

GEORGE	Um... (*An idea occurs to him.*) Well, the garden at dawn. Obviously! You start with the lights down. (*He switches the lights off. It is effectively dark.*) Perhaps some bird song. The beginnings of the dawn chorus. (*Unseen,* BEN *begins to crawl across the stage to the hall.*) You can almost feel the morning dew on your toes! And, ever so slowly, a faint red glow ... The sun begins it's ... inexorable ...
	(YVETTE *enters from the house and switches the lights on.*)
YVETTE	Oh! Excusez moi!
	(BEN *is crouched on all fours in the middle of the room, his farce trousers around his ankles. Pause. Tableau. Finally, he moos like a cow. Pause.* BEN *gets up, pulls up his trousers and shrugs.*)
BEN	I'm not really an actor, but that's basically ...
GEORGE	Yes, well done! Very good! Although I'm not ... entirely sure. I mean, obviously! If you switch to a garden for your final act. You're destroying the er ... Feydeauesque Home-Hotel-Home structure.
BEN	Yes. That's true. Well, anyway! I must go! (*Checks his watch.*) I have a psychopath waiting for me.
	(CHRISTINE *staggers in from the house.*)
ALAN	Jesus!
	(ALAN *rushes to her aid. She collapses into his arms.* BEN *exits quickly to the hall.*)
ALAN	(*to* BEN) Hey! (*To* GEORGE.) What's going on here?!

GEORGE	I've no idea.
CHRISTINE	I feel sick.
ALAN	For Christ's sake . . . (*He carries* CHRISTINE *towards the hall.*) Your friend's in big trouble!
GEORGE	Right. I'll tell him. If I see him again.

(ALAN *and* CHRISTINE *exit, followed by* YVETTE. *Pause.*)

ANNE	What was she doing here?
GEORGE	(*pause*) Um . . .
ANNE	I've suffered enough. If you have one *ounce* of integrity in your soul, you will not lie to me now.

(*Pause.* GEORGE *considers his options.*)

GEORGE	I slept with her. Yes. But only once.

(*Pause.*)

ANNE	Have there been others? (*Beat.*) No. Forget it. I don't want to know. (*Beat.*) I just want out of this. This hopeless marriage. I've wasted too many years already. I just want to go. With some . . . semblance of dignity. (*She takes a deep breath and moves to leave. After a few dignified steps towards the door, she returns to the table.*) And you can go get your own fucking bread!

(*She launches a violent attack on the loaf of sliced bread.* GEORGE *watches, immobile, as she takes out all her aggression on the bread. She destroys the loaf then breaks down. She stands, sobbing.* GEORGE *moves to comfort her but she raises a hand to keep him away. She sits slowly and sobs into her hands. Finally, she takes a breath and begins wiping her tears away.* GEORGE *sits opposite, suffering. He takes what he thinks is a handkerchief from his pocket and hands it to her. She dabs at her eyes with* CHRISTINE'S *knickers but then realises what they are. She stops crying abruptly and holds them up for inspection. Pause.*)

GEORGE I have absolutely no idea . . .

ANNE Shut up. (*Beat.*) Just get out.

(*Pause.* GEORGE *gets up, removes his smoking jacket and throws it scornfully onto the floor. He exits to the house. Pause.* DAVID *enters. He sees the jacket on the floor in his path and picks it up.*)

DAVID Well, I'm off, so . . .

ANNE I'll give you a lift.

DAVID Are you all right?

(*Pause. She stares at the knickers as if she can't believe their existence.*)

ANNE (*big breath*) He admits to screwing that bimbo. I tell him I want a divorce. Then, for some reason, I'm crying my eyes out. So he hands me what he thinks is a handkerchief! (*She holds up the knickers.* DAVID *smiles.*) It's not funny.

DAVID No. Sorry. (*Beat.*) But it's not a bad ending. Is it?

ANNE What?

DAVID First two acts about Feydeau, then third act set in the present. A writer writing about Feydeau. But the story sort of continues. So you keep your Home-Hotel-Home structure.

	(*Rather pleased with himself, he tries the jacket on for size.*)
ANNE	(*incensed*) You're as bad as him! I'm confiding in you about the collapse of my marriage and you just think it's a funny ending for a stupid play!
DAVID	It would be revenge though. Wouldn't it? (*Indicates the script on the table.*) Steal his script. (*Beat.*) He stole it from me anyway.
ANNE	I'm not interested in revenge. It's so primitive.
DAVID	Okay.
ANNE	I refuse to sink to his level.
DAVID	All right. (*Beat.*) Shall we go?
ANNE	(*beat*) Give me a minute.

(*Pause. DAVID exits to the hall. ANNE looks wistfully around the room. Her eyes rest finally on the script. She picks it up and begins flicking through it. We hear the end of the Ravel 'Perpetuum Mobile' piece again. It builds in volume as she reads. As the movement reaches its climax, she takes a deep breath, gathers up all the pages and marches out to the hall. Blackout.*)

The end.

MONKEY'S UNCLE
First published in 2005
by Josef Weinberger Ltd
12-14 Mortimer Street, London, W1T 3JJ
www.josef-weinberger.com

Copyright © 2005 by David Lewis

The author asserts his moral right to be identified as the author of the work.

ISBN 0 85676 290 3

This play is protected by Copyright. According to Copyright Law, no public performance or reading of a protected play or part of that play may be given without prior authorisation from Josef Weinberger Plays, as agent for the Copyright Owners. From time to time it is necessary to restrict or even withdraw the rights of certain plays. **It is therefore essential to check with us before making a commitment to produce a play.**

NO PERFORMANCE MAY BE GIVEN WITHOUT A LICENCE

AMATEUR PRODUCTIONS
Royalties are due at least one calendar month prior to the first performance. A royalty quotation will be issued upon receipt of the following details:

Name of Licensee
Play Title
Place of Performance
Dates and Number of Performances
Audience Capacity
Ticket Prices

PROFESSIONAL PRODUCTIONS
All enquiries regarding professional rights should be addressed to Peters, Fraser and Dunlop Group Ltd, Drury House, 34-43 Russell Street, London WC2B 5HA.

OVERSEAS PRODUCTIONS
Applications for productions overseas should be addressed to our local authorised agents. Further details are listed in our catalogue of plays, published every two years, or available from Josef Weinberger Plays at the address above.

CONDITIONS OF SALE
This book is sold subject to the condition that it shall not by way of trade or otherwise be resold, hired out, circulated or distributed without prior consent of the Publisher. **Reproduction of the text either in whole or part and by any means is strictly forbidden.**

Printed by Biddles Ltd, King's Lynn, Norfolk